PAUL G. BEIDLER

D0497613

Frames in James: *The Tragic Muse, The Turn of the Screw, What Maisie Knew,* and *The Ambassadors*

N 8 ELS Monograph Series

PAUL G. BEIDLER

Frames in James: *The Tragic Muse*, *The Turn of the Screw*, *What Maisie Knew*, and *The Ambassadors*

Saint Peter's University Library
Withdrawn

ELS

English Literary Studies
University of Victoria
1993

ENGLISH LITERARY STUDIES
Published at the University of Victoria

FOUNDER AND GENERAL EDITOR
Samuel L. Macey

EDITORIAL BOARD
Patricia J. Köster
Victor A. Neufeldt
Terry G. Sherwood
Reginald C. Terry

ADVISORY EDITORS
David Fowler, *University of Washington*
Donald Greene, *University of Southern California*
Juliet McMaster, *University of Alberta*
Richard J. Schoeck, *University of Colorado*
Arthur Sherbo, *Michigan State University*

BUSINESS MANAGER
Hedy Miller

ISBN 0-920604-70-6

The ELS Monograph Series is published in consultation with members of the Department by ENGLISH LITERARY STUDIES, Department of English, University of Victoria, B.C., Canada, V8W 3P4.

ELS Monograph Series No. 59
© 1993 by Paul G. Beidler

PS
2124
.B42
1993

For Aphrodite

The truth is that what a happy thought has to give depends immensely on the general turn of the mind capable of it, and on the fact that its loyal entertainer, cultivating fondly its possible relations and extensions, the bright efflorescence latent in it, but having to take other things in their order too, is terribly at the mercy of his mind. That organ has only to exhale, in its degree, a fostering tropic air in order to produce complications almost beyond reckoning. The trap laid for his superficial convenience resides in the fact that, though the relations of a human figure or a social occurrence are what make such objects interesting, they also make them, to the same tune, difficult to isolate, to surround with the sharp black line, to frame in the square, the circle, the charming oval, that helps any arrangement of objects to become a picture.

HENRY JAMES, Preface to *The Awkward Age.*

What you want to do—going against the feast—is not to mix genres but to extend metaphors. You can always try: question of style.

JACQUES DERRIDA, *The Truth in Painting.*

CONTENTS

ACKNOWLEDGEMENTS

I am indebted to James R. Frakes, who introduced me to James, for his enthusiasm, and to Gordon Bearn, with whom I first encountered the work of Jacques Derrida. I could never have completed this project without the encouragement of my wife Aphrodite, and I also thank my father Peter G. Beidler, whose example I shall always follow as best I can, and Jan Hunin and Scott Mastroianni, who helped during the revision stages of this book.

ABBREVIATIONS

Abbreviations of titles by Henry James and Jacques Derrida used in this volume:

AA	*The Awkward Age*
AN	*The Art of the Novel*
CT	*The Complete Tales of Henry James*
D	*Dissemination*
G	*Of Grammatology*
LC	*Henry James: Literary Criticism*
NB	*The Complete Notebooks of Henry James*
TA	*The Ambassadors*
TM	*The Tragic Muse*
TP	*The Truth in Painting*
TS	*The Turn of the Screw*
WD	*The Wings of the Dove*
WMK	*What Maisie Knew*

PREFACE

Henry James's essay "The Art of Fiction," a critique of another essay of the same name by Sir Walter Besant,[1] argues that the novel as an art form is free of all standards and subject to no set of requirements that critics may wish to impose upon it. James was against an exact method or science of fiction, and his only advice to a pupil who might ask for the rudiments of writing a novel, he claims, would be "'Ah, well, you must do it as you can!'" (*LC* 50):

> The only obligation to which in advance we may hold a novel, without incurring the accusation of being arbitrary, is that it be interesting. That general responsibility rests upon it, but it is the only one I can think of. (*LC* 49)

James's project in "The Art of Fiction" is to show that fiction is not a craft but as fine an art as painting, and his vehicle for communicating this message is his insistence upon "the analogy between the art of the painter and the art of the novelist" (*LC* 46), an analogy he sees as complete. He argues that painting and philosophy are the "sister art[s]" of fiction (*LC* 46):

> it seems to me to give [the novelist] a great character, the fact that he has at once so much in common with the philosopher and the painter; this double analogy is his magnificent heritage. (*LC* 47)

Like a painting, James writes, the novel simply "stands there before you, in the honesty of pink and green and a gilt frame" (*LC* 48).

The premise of the present essay is simply that this analogy is worth exploring in James's own work: a philosophical analysis of the Jamesian novel as painting ought to prove to be a profitable one. James's fascination with the marginal and the subordinate makes the application of the Derridian aesthetic seem especially pertinent, and particularly relevant is Jacques Derrida's essay "Parergon" in *The Truth in Painting*, a deconstruction of Kant's implied hierarchy of work over frame in the third *Critique*. Traditional aesthetics has assumed a hierarchy in which the painting, the work of art, is of primary importance and its frame only of secondary interest. This hierarchy is inverted time after time in Derrida's essays, where attention is focused on the frame rather than the painting, the preface rather than the book, and the marginal rather than the primary.[2]

The parergon, briefly, is a specific case of the supplement, the foundation of Derrida's *Of Grammatology*. In this seminal deconstruction of Rousseau's conception of writing "as a supplement to speech" (*G* 144) Derrida describes the logic of the supplement and its two significations as follows:

> The supplement adds itself, it is a surplus, a plenitude enriching another plenitude, the *fullest measure* of presence. It cumulates and accumulates presence. It is thus that art, *technè*, image representation, convention, etc., come as supplements to nature and are rich with this entire cumulating function. This kind of supplementarity determines in a certain way all the conceptual oppositions within which Rousseau inscribes the notion of Nature to the extent that it *should* be self-sufficient.
>
> But the supplement supplements. It adds only to replace. It intervenes or insinuates itself *in-the-place-of*; if it fills, it is as if one fills a void. If it represents and makes an image, it is by the anterior default of a presence. Compensatory and vicarious, the supplement is an adjunct, a sub-altern insistence which *takes-(the)-place*. As a substitute, it is not simply added to the positivity of a presence, it produces no relief, its place is assigned in the structure by the mark of emptiness. Somewhere, something can be filled up *of itself*, can accomplish itself, only by allowing itself to be filled through sign and proxy. The sign is always the supplement of the thing itself. (*G* 144-45)

The supplement is a substitution that is necessitated by a lack: Derrida shows that Rousseau's Mamma is a supplement to mother nature, that his Thérèse is a supplement to Mamma, and that masturbation is a supplement to Thérèse. To Rousseau, of course, there is no substitute for a mother's love, and so the supplement is evil, but to Derrida this supplementation merely constitutes a chain of signifiers with no signified, another example of his "axial proposition" that "there is nothing outside the text" (*G* 163). The notion of the supplement is analogous to that of the "Outwork" or preface in *Dissemination* and that of the parergon, or frame, in *The Truth in Painting*.

To Derrida, a painting is not a unit but a composite of work and frame in which the frame, ostensibly subordinate to the work, is actually of primary importance because of the extent to which it is subordinate—the extent, in other words, to which it is necessitated by the work. In short, the frame does real work:

> The frame labors indeed. Place of labor, structurally bordered origin of surplus value, i.e., overflowed on these two borders by what it overflows, it gives indeed. Like wood. It creaks and cracks, breaks down and dislocates

> even as it cooperates in the production of the product, overflows it and is deduc(t)ed from it. (*TP* 75)

The parergon is like a wheelchair that a decrepit geriatric might use to remain mobile:

> If things run as though on wheels, this is perhaps because things aren't going so well, by reason of an internal infirmity in the thesis which demands to be supplemented by a prosthesis or only ensures the progress of the exposition with the aid of a wheelchair of a child's pushchair. Thus one pushes forward something which cannot stand up, does not erect itself by itself. Framing always supports and contains that which, by itself, collapses forthwith, exc (*TP* 78-79)

The work, Derrida claims, collapses without the frame. The range of this metaphor is wittily obfuscated by one of the many blank boxes that periodically interrupt "Parergon", made up as it is of "Fragments detached (unframed) from the course of an exposition" (*TP* 16). The fragment "exc" here (*s'exc* in French) must be the first half either of "except" or "exclude," which seems to indicate that there are some cases in which the work does not necessarily collapse without the frame, but whatever qualification once followed is gone; Derrida's concern is with those works that do require framing. I will show here that to a great extent James's was as well.

The frame has come to be intimately associated with our notion of what a painting is, and Derrida's premise that certain works of art somehow need to be framed involves an irony basic to my analysis: it assumes that the work is intrinsically incapable of doing its own work. The importance of Derrida's theory of the parergon to literary criticism lies in the fact that the incapability of attaining true primacy (or complete presence) and the need to somehow overcome this handicap by juxtaposition with an "other" are characteristics of both the work of art and the human spirit.[3] Henry James was clearly sensitive to this relationship between ergon and parergon, both in structuring his novels (most notably, of course, the *Turn of the Screw*) and in portraying the human relationships within them. His interest in the subordinate and the charm of the vague produced such characters as Little Bilham and Sir Claude, who are attractive precisely because they never seem to do anything, and such formidable creations as Mrs. Newsome and Lionel Croy, who exemplify the power of impotence properly framed. Lambert Strether, John Marcher, and the governess in *The Turn of the Screw*, likewise, are all personages who see and wait but rarely act and whose fates are determined by their interpretation of events more than by their actions. James is thus to be compared with Derrida here on the basis of his interest in the significance and beauty of the passive and the subordinate—the novel itself was a subordinate genre that James was instrumental in raising to the level of a fine art.

Three main characteristics of the frame can be gleaned from Derrida's "Parergon," as I will show in Chapter II:

1. It exists beside the work, neither part of it nor detachable from it—it is an "ill-detachable detachment" (*TP* 59) [the first signification];
2. It either stands out as a "bold figure," forcing both the work and the wall on which it is hung into a background in which they blur together like ocean and sky, or it disappears completely;
3. It redresses a lacuna, a lack in the work that cannot or must not be filled [the second signification].[4]

In this study I deal with four manifestations of the parergon in James's oeuvre. First is the literal frame as it operates within the narrative: in *The Tragic Muse* Miriam Rooth, herself a work of art, "a producer whose production is her own person," transcends the frame imposed upon her by her profession and her audience. In doing so she becomes, both for the reader and for the other characters in the story, a work of sublime modernist realism. Miriam brings life into the confines of the frame and thereby castrates it, nullifying its false division of the world into the categories of 'art' and 'life.' The Prologue to *The Turn of the Screw*, which occupies my second chapter, is itself a frame, and in this work the dynamics of the drama are subjected to intense experimentation. The Prologue is a complete and effective frame tale that fits Derrida's notion of the parergon, working to redress the lack of a beginning in the governess's narrative and framing romance with drama. My point in Chapter III is that the frame/work relationship can be found in relations between people in the realm of fiction as well as between elements of a work of art. In *What Maisie Knew*, Maisie Farange is herself a parergonal frame, used to compensate for the lack of decency in her parents' adulterous relationships, and the primacy of the frame is as peculiar a characteristic within the work as it is outside it. In *The Ambassadors*, finally, the frame as structural device and the parergonal nature of the hero are combined. The Lambinet chapters (30-31) form a parergonal frame that contains the great revelation of the truth, a truth that is both necessary in a portrait of a "man of imagination" and incommensurable with the genre of realism. This novel is in a sense the ultimate utilization of the dynamics of the parergon: *The Ambassadors* has its climax in its frame, and my Chapter IV is an exploration of this design.

This essay is a tribute to the importance of the painting metaphor in James's fiction. If my application of Derrida's methods has not lead, by any means, to 'the truth in James,' it has proved to be "a theory which would run along as if on wheels" (*TP* 53), and as such it is as much a tribute to Derrida as to James.

P.G.B.
Toronto, Spring 1993

CHAPTER I

The Tragic Muse: Fiction and Realism

> *Colossal (kolossalich)* thus qualifies the presentation, the putting on stage or into presence, the catching-sight, rather, of some thing, but of something which is not a thing, since it is a concept. Nor simply unpresentable: almost unpresentable. And by reason of its size: it is "almost too large." This concept is announced and then eludes presentation on the stage. One would say, by reason of its excessive size, that it was obscene.
>
> Jacques Derrida, *Parergon*[1]

James describes *The Tragic Muse* in the New York Preface as "a story about art" (*AN* 81) but more aptly, later in the same piece, as "a picture of some of the personal consequences of the art-appetite raised to intensity" (*AN* 90). It is primarily a story of an actress named Miriam Rooth and her ascent to fame and glory on the London stage, but the problem with it has always been that it has two plots: it also traces events in the life of a young politician named Nick Dormer who renounces his seat in the House of Commons to become a portrait painter. Marriage is the most convenient way of uniting two plots in a novel, and Peter Sherringham, Nick's cousin and a "rising young diplomat," tries to effect such a union. Sherringham falls in love with Miriam Rooth and tries to persuade her to give up the stage and marry him, but in the end she repudiates him and quietly marries Basil Dashwood, her undistinguished manager. The two plots are finally fused together, however, not by the diplomat Peter Sherringham, who disappears to a remote post in Central America in a futile attempt to escape Miriam's power over him, but by the politician-turned-artist Nick Dormer himself, who paints two portraits of Miriam. Unity is achieved, then, not through life but through art, or rather, as I will show, through life within art. These two portraits, which unify both the two separate stories that make up the novel and the two arts of painting and drama, are the focus of the present chapter. These paintings show James's sublime heroine developing in the novel from an actress, a mere art object, to a woman and a work of modernist realism. In doing so, of course, Miriam elevates both drama and the novel itself from base forms of entertainment to high art. James writes in the Preface to the novel that he wanted to "'do something about art'" (*AN* 79) and that "the conflict between art and 'the world'" was one of his "half-dozen great primary motives" in writing *The Tragic Muse* (*AN* 79). I will discuss this conflict between art and life as it relates to another fundamental conflict in the novel, that between fiction and realism.

The Tragic Muse opens with a sketch of a group of dull English people in Paris. They are in the sculpture garden of the Palais d'Industrie, which one might suppose to be a lively place around noon, but the people appear bored both with life and with the art that surrounds them. They are expressionless and morose ("dressed in mourning" [*TM* 8]), and even their name, "Dormer," suggests blank drowsiness. The English travelers are, as it turns out, "a rigid English family" (*TM* 17), but they are more a family of statues than of people. More like sculptured busts than living connoisseurs, they are lifeless objects that together form what the narrator calls "a successful plastic fact" (*TM* 7). The Dormers are "finished productions" (*TM* 8), and the perfect irony of the opening scene is that while they seem bored with art they hilariously echo the busts around them:

> The fresh, diffused light of the Salon made them clear and important; they were finished productions, in their way, and ranged there motionless on their green bench, they were almost as much on exhibition as if they had been hung on the line. (*TM* 8)

James's subjects are as "clear," "important," and "motionless" as the statues in the garden. They are "interesting" in their expressionless "taciturnity" (*TM* 8): Nick's sister Biddy is "herself an English picture" (*TM* 28), and Lady Agnes's head is admired as if it were a detached hunk of clay on a pedestal:

> This competent matron, acquainted evidently with grief, but not weakened by it, had a high forehead, to which the quality of the skin gave a singular polish—it glittered even when seen at a distance; a nose which achieved a high free curve; and a tendency to throw back her head and carry it well above her, as if to disengage it from the rest of her person. (*TM* 8-9).

Lady Agnes's "white triangular forehead" (*TM* 9) and the "high free curve" of her nose seem to be her only souvenirs from her life at the dubious "Castle Nugent" (*TM* 54). We are warned by the dialogue between Nick and Biddy that follows this opening still life that the analogy between human heads and clay ones is neither simple nor merely satirical in *The Tragic Muse.* The traditional relationship between art and the world is being questioned here: instead of art imitating life, life is being shown to imitate art. This reversal is clearly an ironic one. James's method was to blur the common distinction between art and life from the start of the story by portraying his actors and actresses as statuary. In doing so he creates a world in which people seem static and dead while art comes alive. This resemblance between the people and the statues is enforced from the first line of the novel, where by describing the English travelers as "perpendicular" and "speechless" the narrator compares them with the art objects themselves:

> The people of France have made it no secret that those of England, as a general thing, are to their perception, an inexpressive and speechless race, perpendicular and unsociable, unaddicted to enriching any bareness of contact with verbal or other embroidery. (*TM* 7)

But we get the impression here that if they are art objects they are unfinished ones, unenriched by "embroidery." They are backgrounds, canvasses without stitching or paint. In short, they are neither art nor life but something vague in between.

The effect here is an aesthetic and ontological uncertainty: we expect the Dormers to be either artistic or, if we find the novel absorbing enough, real, but the terms that the narrator uses to describe them prevents us from so categorizing them. The opposition of art and life is deconstructed, and the uncertainty manifests itself in two of the most peculiar aspects of the beginning of *The Tragic Muse.* First, this uncertainty is the reason for James's decision to set aside the unity of the central consciousness, the absence of which he had a "mortal horror" (*AN* 83). The result is a duality, a division of the whole into subject and object. James replaced the subjective central consciousness in *The Tragic Muse* with what Alan W. Bellringer calls an "objective centre" (Bellringer 78) in order to emphasize this division. Though Miriam is the "subject" of the novel, we see her only through the eyes of the others. The narrator is a "foreign observer" (*TM* 17) who distances us as readers from the characters at the same time that he tells us her story, and this distance makes them less realistic—the central consciousness, which has been called the fourth unity, is usually the essence of James's realism—and more artistic. This uncertainty could not have been achieved by central consciousness narration,[2] which produces ambiguity that is subjective, not objective.

In the Preface James recalls being uncomfortable with this division of subject and object that necessitated the division of the novel into plot and subplot:

SAINT PETER'S COLLEGE LIBRARY
JERSEY CITY, NEW JERSEY 07306

A story was a story, a picture a picture, and I had a mortal horror of two stories, two pictures in one. The reason of this was the clearest—my subject was immediately, under that disadvantage, so cheated of its indispensable centre as to become of no more use than a wheel without a hub is of use for moving a cart. (*AN* 83-84)

James was determined, however, to fuse the two halves of his "monster" (*AN* 84) into a harmonious whole, and this unity had to be accomplished through Miriam Rooth herself. Miriam's primary attribute, as we will see, is her objecthood[3]—Sherringham is stung by her "histrionic hardness" (*TM* 555), and she is a "concretion" in the Preface (*AN* 91)—and it is this objecthood that prevents us from ever seeing things from her perspective: we could do this, the narrator explains,

only if it were open to us to regard this young lady through some other medium than the mind of her friends. We have chosen, as it happens, for some of the advantages it carries with it, the indirect vision . . . (*TM* 321)

The central consciousness is replaced in the novel by a central object, one of which we are only allowed an "indirect vision," and it is the absence of this central object that is primarily felt in the first chapter of the novel. Since Miriam is missing in the first chapter and the first half of the second, the "famous centre of one's subject" (*AN* 89) in the early chapters of the novel is simply this aesthetic uncertainty itself. The early pages constitute a situation that is only unified by the absence of substance and the resulting aesthetic uncertainty. The beginning of the novel can thus be seen as a frame with no picture: the frame is presented before Miriam, the image, arrives to occupy it. The tension we feel derives from this lack of a central image, the lack of Miriam Rooth.

The ontological uncertainty of the opening pages also results in the fact that James, while he gives us no character in the story for whom art is irrelevant or unimportant, seems to be presenting every type of person connected with the art world except the artist—the only exceptions are Nick and Miriam Rooth, who only become artists toward the end of the novel.[4] The beginning of *The Tragic Muse* is teeming with art but without an artist, just as it is teeming with representations[5] and images but devoid of living, realistic inhabitants. The reader is confronted with three different attitudes toward art and life, none of which seems appropriate to "a dramatic picture of the artist-life" (*AN* 70): Lady Agnes simply despises all art as vulgar illusion,[6] Nick worships it but has given up all active participation in it, and Gabriel Nash, one of Nick's old college friends, has both absorbed it and trivialized it. Biddy Dormer, who simply wants to be an artist, is thus understandably confused by the conflict of attitudes around her, and the reader may be justified in sharing her confusion. James's characters worship art, collect it, discriminate amongst it or despise it, but because they cannot create it they can never escape it. And in their inaction they resemble it more and more—they are held in suspension between art and life, on the border between the two categories.

But Miriam Rooth does not immediately fill the void upon her appearance in the second chapter and assume her role as the novel's "objective centre." She emerges with her mother under the auspices of Gabriel Nash—they are his "queer female appendages" (*TM* 28). Miriam Rooth and Gabriel Nash are each enigmatic non-artists, Nash because he refuses to do anything and Miriam because she has never yet done anything, and because they both claim to be artists it is not immediately clear which of them will fill the void.[7] They are polar opposites, each representing an alternative that the other characters in the story, especially Peter and Nick, must either accept or renounce. Two possible resolutions to the ambiguous relationship between art and life are thus presented concurrently to Biddy and her brother amid the statues. I will discuss them in the order that they appear.

Gabriel Nash, who appears first, may be described as the incarnation of the absence of substance. He represents an extremist aesthetic model that Nick chooses to follow immediately. Nash claims that "we must feel everything, everything that we can. We are here for that" (*TM* 28). Nash, who has written "a sort of novel" (*TM* 27), is presented unmistakably as an artist figure; to Biddy he seems to "draw rich effects and wandering airs from [the English language]—to modulate and manipulate it as he would have done a musical instrument" (*TM* 23). Like Nick and Biddy, however, he feels passionately about art but never produces any, but he is different from them in that he has made his impotence a doctrine, a way of life. When Biddy asks him "Are you an æsthete?" he responds:

> "Ah, there's one of the formulas! That's walking in one's hat! . . . As I say, I keep to the simplest way. I find that gives one enough to do. Merely to be is such a *métier*, to live is such an art, to feel is such a career!" (*TM* 31)

Gabriel simply exists, but he claims to do so in a way that is artistic. He represents taste without action, and as a result his only actions are negative; he becomes a work of "the art of life" (*TM* 31), one to be admired not for what he does but for what he does not do, for what he is, and, most importantly, for what he feels:

> "My only generalizations are my actions."
> "We shall see *them*, then."

"Ah, excuse me. You can't see them with the naked eye. Moreover, mine are principally negative. People's actions, I know, are, for the most part, the things they do, but mine are all the things I don't do. There are so many of those, so many, but they don't produce any effect. And the rest are shades—extremely fine shades."

"Shades of behaviour?" Nick inquired, with an interest which surprised his sister; Mr. Nash's discourse striking her mainly as the twaddle of the underworld.

"Shades of impression, of appreciation," said the young man, with his explanatory smile. "My only behaviour is my feelings." (*TM* 29)

In claiming to produce no effect Nash sets up his opposition to Miriam, whose effect, as I will show, is her art: "I shall only be," he maintains till the end (*TM* 596). Art and life are fused together in his person; he has replaced the artist as the link between them, or so he would have us believe, and it is in this sense that he seems to represent a resolution of the art/life ambiguity. Nash is a critic, one traditionally subordinate to the artist but who, like many modern critics, has promoted himself to a primary rank. His philosophy, according to which criticism is more noble than creation, is encapsulated in his rejection of the world, contaminated as it is with "the grossness of choice" (*TM* 60) or, as James later put it, "the grossness of reality" (*LC* 1207).

Nash is thus present throughout the book as an almost supernatural entity, a puzzling annoyance to some and an ideal to others. His poignant wit makes him a constant presence in the novel, a fascination and an itch—Nick adores him and Julia finds him repulsive. His lack of substance, however, prevents him from ever attaining real significance in a community of art-lovers. This lack of substance is underlined by the fact that he is not even mentioned in James's Preface to the novel—it is as if he is eventually forgotten even by his own creator. In the end Nash disappears "'without a trace,' like a personage in a fairy-tale or a melodrama" (*TM* 597). But through his negative actions he achieves complete and positive presence in the novel. As a result he is like a ghost that seems to appear and disappear at will:

He emerged out of vagueness (his Sicily might have been the Sicily of "A Winter's Tale"), and would evidently be reabsorbed in it; but his presence was positive and pervasive enough. He was very lively while he lasted. (*TM* 305)

Nash's significance must be neither overstated nor ignored. He represents the culmination of the static, artless life; he is a rigid Englishman made beautiful.

Nash represents the act of being; for him "Being is doing" (*TM* 308), and for Miriam, by contrast, doing is being. Miriam, who is as much something as Nash is nothing, is an actress, one who acts and whose actions constitute her being in its entirety—"whose only being was to make believe" (*TM* 150). Nash concentrates on being and ceases to exist, but Miriam, who focuses on action, attains objecthood. As Peter Sherringham notes at a party he throws to display her to his friends,

> it was inevitable to treat her position as connected with the principal place on the carpet, with silence and attention and the pulling together of chairs. (*TM* 113)

Like Gabriel she is an artist of sorts, and like him also she is a work of art at the same time, one that Nash later even claims as his own: "I invented her, I introduced her, I revealed her" (*TM* 314). Miriam is more than the "objective centre" of the novel—she is actually an object—"the plastic quality of her person was the only sign of a vocation" (*TM* 105). She is thus opposed to Nash as pure substance is to a vacuum.

Miriam, as an object, has a much more powerful "effect" (*TM* 276) on those around her than Nash does, and this effect is crucial to my reading of the novel. She is portrayed through the observations of those who look upon her as more resembling art than life, but her appearance makes the others want to produce, to do things—she excites "the pulling together of chairs." Miriam distinguishes herself from the others, including Nash, by subordinating them, as she does with Biddy that first day in the sculpture garden:

> Biddy [on first seeing Miriam] had a momentary sense of being a figure in a ballet, a dramatic ballet—a subordinate, motionless figure, to be dashed at, to music, or capered up to. It would be a very dramatic ballad indeed if this person were the heroine. (*TM* 25)

Miriam is the heroine of this "ballet" because she has the effect of animating those around her.[8] She makes them frame her, unifying them by subordinating them and thereby transforming them from a group of lifeless busts into the background of a ballet or drama of which she is the main character. Though she is herself as "plastic" (*TM* 168) as those around her, she is also alive in a way that they are not: she lives through her effect. Miriam, like Henry St George in "The Lesson of the Master," makes others want to act, "to try something" (*TM* 319), and through her actions and the actions she inspires in others she achieves life through plasticity. She inspires art as well as life: Nick offers to paint her at their first meeting—"'I should like to paint her portrait; she's made for that'" (*TM* 97), he tells her mother, and Biddy soon wants to sculpt her head (*TM* 115) (Julia Dallow snidely admits that though she's "dreadfully vulgar" "she'd do for that" [*TM* 122]). Nash wants to watch her and Peter, to whom "she seemed so 'plastic'" (*TM* 69), wants to marry her. She is an object, and yet at the same time she is the only one among them who seems to be alive.

As the novel's title implies, the ambiguities in the conflict between art and life are resolved not by Nash the ethereal critic but by Miriam Rooth, a strange fusion of object with action, and they are resolved in the theater, the place where art and life are most happily fused together. Gabriel Nash and Miriam Rooth are both actors (see *TM* 165), and they represent being and doing respectively, two alternative ways of avoiding the ontological quagmire that the other characters, particularly Peter and Nick, find themselves caught in as the story begins. Neither alternative is ever finally excluded, hence the essential disjointedness of the novel: Peter chooses Miriam but disappears into oblivion with Nash while Nick, after renouncing the world as Nash advises him to do, begins like Miriam to learn "the beauty of obstinacy" (*TM* 497). Nash's solution to the problem of the ambiguity of life is less valid for James but more fascinating—it evolved, over the course of James's life, into what I will later call the Paris aesthetic (see Chapter IV). The being/doing dilemma demands not a choice or a renunciation but a fusion. This fusion is accomplished by Miriam Rooth, who forces herself into a position of primacy and to whose brilliance the others, willingly or not, must act as a frame.

The choices that Nick and Peter make between Gabriel Nash and Miriam Rooth are clearly based on aesthetic judgment, and they make their choices on the basis of more fundamental choices between the beautiful and the sublime. Peter Sherringham follows Miriam because he is in love with her, but it is not so much his attraction to her as the nature of his desperate actions that needs to be explained. Peter Sherringham is confused about Miriam Rooth, "the Tragic Muse" who gives James's longest novel its title, from beginning to end. He finds her person irresistible but her profession, that of an actress, almost nauseatingly vulgar:

> But what was she, the priestess ["of art"], when one came to think of it, but a female gymnast, a mountebank at higher wages? She didn't literally hang by her heels from a trapeze, holding a fat man in her teeth, but she made the same use of her tongue, of her eyes, of the imitative trick, that her muscular sister made of leg and jaw. (*TM* 151)

Acting, of course, is pretending, and Peter sees Miriam as a professional liar. But we must see that Miriam Rooth, that "odd animal the artist who happened to have been born a woman" (*TM* 184), is real not only in spite of, but actually because of her talent at representing and imitating.

Peter's life is a search for beauty, and his need for this beauty is clear from almost everything he says to Miriam:

> "Be beautiful—be only that," Sherringham advised. "Be only what you can be so well—something that one may turn to for a glimpse of perfection, to lift one out of all the vulgarities of the day." (*TM* 269)

We may wonder, however, at Sherringham's insistence that Miriam be *only* beautiful, and also at the nature of such a beauty of "perfection" that would seem to exclude all other attributes. The beauty Sherringham is after is a specific kind of beauty, one that is similar to the beauty Immanuel Kant describes in *The Critique of Judgement.* In the "Explication of the Beautiful Inferred from the First Movement" of this *Critique* Kant writes:

> "*Taste* is the ability to judge an object, or a way of presenting it, by means of a liking or disliking *devoid of all interest.* The object of such a liking is called *beautiful.*" (Kant 53)[9]

Kantian beauty is different from the merely agreeable: we like it without having any interest in it or being involved with it. Our lack of interest makes it possible for our judgments to have "subjective universal validity" (Kant 58), which Kant wants to show that aesthetic judgments can have. The Kantian art teacher can thus teach only by example, only by producing art,[10] and can only do so with genius, "the ability to [exhibit] *aesthetic ideas*" (Kant 217). The question of the artist's method is a futile one in this context that results simply in the ontological circle that Heidegger takes up in "The Origin of the Work of Art"[11]—Kant's interest, and Peter Sherringham's too, is in art itself and the full appreciation of it.[12]

Peter's view of beauty, like Kant's, depends upon the nonexistence of the artist, and what he dreams of is an artistless art, one of perfection and disinterested appreciation.[13] While waiting for Miriam and her mother at Balaklava Place the morning after viewing Nick's first painting of Miriam, Peter is "soaring so high . . . that he had almost lost consciousness of the minor differences of earthly things" (*TM* 376). He then has a vision that reveals the grandeur of his illusions about drama:

> Sherringham had, as he went, an intense vision (he had often had it before) of the conditions which were still absent, the great and complete ones, those which would give the girl's talent a superior, glorious stage. More than ever he desired them, mentally invoked them, filled them out in imagination, cheated himself with the idea that they were possible. He saw in them a momentary illusion and confusion: a great academic, artistic theater, subsidized and unburdened with money-getting, rich in its repertory, rich in the high quality and wide array of its servants, and above all in the authority of an impossible

> administrator—a manager personally disinterested, not an actor with an eye to the main chance, pouring fourth a continuity of tradition, striving for perfection, laying a splendid literature under contribution. (*TM* 378-79)

It is not the theater itself that Peter would change so much as its "conditions." He dreams of an art form that would be beautiful in the Kantian sense: he wants an "academic" theater, "subsidized and unburdened," overseen and directed by a "personally disinterested" manager and sustained by "the general encouragement of a thing perfectly done" (*TM* 378). He dreams of an art form that would operate without the interest or profit of anyone involved; the artist would be replaced by an "impossible administrator" and everyone involved would be "decent":

> "You were made to charm and console, to represent beauty and harmony and variety to miserable human beings; the daily life of man is the theater for that—not a vulgar shop with a turnstile, that's only open once in the twenty-four hours." (*TM* 544-45)

Peter wants a theater with these conditions because he craves a form of beauty without interest—one that will not infect its audience with its own vulgarity as the London theater has infected him.

Peter Sherringham is enamored with the idea of a theater that could be appreciated disinterestedly because Miriam, the young actress he wants to form into the main counterpart of this theater, has captured his interest. He is thus involved with the theater now in a way that he was not before because he is in love with her, and this means that he is no longer able to pretend, as he has done in the past, to appreciate the passion of the stage without implicating himself in the vulgar "nudity of the stage" (*TM* 162).[14] Sherringham, then, must form in Miriam Rooth the Kantian beauty of concepts, disinterest, and perfection. The result, were he to succeed in this, would be both a theatrical institution and a heroine—Miriam—with the sort of beauty that Nick Dormer sees in Julia Dallow's "fine head" (*TM* 76):

> Her hair was of so dark a brown that it was commonly regarded as black, and so abundant that a plain arrangement was required to keep it in discrete relation to the rest of her person. Her eyes were of a gray tint that was sometimes pronounced too light; and they were not sunken in her face, but placed well on the surface. Her nose was perfect, but her mouth was too small; and Nick Dormer, and doubtless other persons as well, had sometimes wondered how, with such a mouth, her face could have expressed decision. Her figure helped it, for she looked tall (being extremely slender), though she was not, and her head took turns and positions which, though they were a matter of but half an inch out of the common, this way or that, somehow contributed to the air of resolution and temper. . . . And all together she was beautiful, with the pure

style of her capable head, her hair like darkness, her eyes like early twilight, her mouth like a rare pink flower. (*TM* 76-77)

Julia is "beautiful" in the way that a work of art is beautiful—her eyes are well "placed" and many of her parts are models of perfection. To Nick she is the "embodiment of beauty" (*TM* 301), "a composed picture" (*TM* 207) and to the increasingly poetic Miriam she is "the one—the beauty, the wonderful beauty" (*TM* 583). Although her proportions lack harmony her style is "pure" because her imperfections balance each other and combine with her perfections to create "an air of resolution and temper."[15] Julia, at least as regards her appearance, approximates that "glimpse of perfection," that something "to lift one out of all the vulgarities of the day" that Peter is searching for in Miriam.

Julia's beauty, however, is solely the fortuitous combination of her parts. Her perfections and flaws combine to form a noble countenance of grace and dignity, but Peter clearly has something much more imposing than his sister in mind when he dreams of molding Miriam into a work of art. A more grandiose example of this sort of beauty in *The Tragic Muse*, seen again through Nick's eyes, is Notre Dame cathedral:

> "Ah, the beautiful—there it stands, over there!" said Nick Dormer. . . . Notre Dame *is* solid; Notre Dame *is* wise, on Notre Dame the distracted mind can rest. Come over and look at her!" . . . "How it straightens things out and blows away one's vapours—anything that's *done!*" (TM 139)

Peter has in mind something of the grandeur of the great cathedral when he begs Miriam to be beautiful. The similarities between Miriam Rooth and Notre Dame are many and significant. Miriam, as we have seen, seems also to look down on mortal man from on high as Notre Dame does:

> They came out before the church, which looks down on a square where the past, once so thick in the very heart of Paris, has been made rather a blank, pervaded, however, by the everlasting freshness of the great cathedral-face. (*TM* 139)

Miriam, too, animates her landscape in the same way that the cathedral pervades the city with "everlasting freshness." Peter craves the kind of innocent beauty that Nick sees around him, and he searches for this beauty in the theater.

One of the problems with Peter's need to make Miriam beautiful, at least according to Kant's definition of beauty, is that he is very much interested in her, but another is that she is actually rather plain; in fact, those who see her off the stage seem to be more disturbed than enamored by her appearance. Biddy is the first to notice her strange arresting posture among the statues while Nick and Gabriel are getting reacquainted:

> Her arms hung at her sides, her head was bent, her face lowered, so that she had the odd appearance of raising her eyes from under her brows; and in this attitude she was striking, though her air was unconciliatory, almost dangerous. (*TM* 25)

Miriam's head, like many in *The Tragic Muse*, is constantly admired—often as if it were a sculptured bust on a pedestal in a museum.[16] But Miriam's beauty is more a construction of Peter's fancy than a quality she actually possesses. Unlike Julia's, Miriam's head is not beautiful at all:

> The expression that came nearest to belonging to her, as it were, was the one that came nearest to being a blank—an air of inanity when she forgot herself, watching something. Then her eye was heavy and her mouth rather common; though it was perhaps just at such a moment that the fine line of her head told most. She had looked slightly *bête* even when Sherringham, on their first meeting at Madame Carré's, said to Nick Dormer that she was the image of the Tragic Muse. (*TM* 151)

Miriam's features are dull, her expression, though telling, is "blank," and she is "*bête.*"[17] But she is also somehow, at the same time, in Sherringham's estimation "the image of the Tragic Muse," and we may wonder how this is possible. The answer, I think, is that Miriam Rooth is to be regarded as neither a *femme du monde* nor a work of art but as a fusion or synthesis of the two categories, a synthesis that I will call realism. Peter seems unable to grasp this synthesis, observing her as if she were actually made of clay:

> . . . he had the impression that she might do what she liked with her face. It was an elastic substance, an element of gutta-percha, like the flexibility of the gymnast, the lady who, at a music-hall, is shot from the mouth of a cannon. He coloured a little at this quickened view of the actress; he had always looked more poetically, somehow, at that priestess of art. (*TM* 151)

Peter sees Miriam as both "priestess of art" and "a contortionist at a county fair" (*TM* 554), and he is unable to resolve this paradox: to him each category excludes the other. But she is both priestess and gymnast, just as she is both the artist and the art work, "a producer whose production is her own person" (*TM* 438). Her ability to play both roles is what frustrates Sherringham. He "coloured" because he wants to see her as a poem, an image, and he is confounded by her plain plasticity. Beauty is a quality that Miriam simply does not possess.

A beautiful object is something we like disinterestedly, but "the liking for the sublime," Kant writes, "contains not so much a positive pleasure as rather admiration and respect, and so should be called a negative pleasure" (Kant 98). What Peter feels in Miriam's presence is this negative pleasure. The sublime is a negative, contrapurposive pleasure—it is a feeling of the subject, not an attribute of the object, and it is thus appropriate to a novel with an "objective centre." Kant writes:

> In presenting the sublime in nature the mind feels *agitated*. . . . This agitation (above all at its inception) can be compared with a vibration, i.e with a rapid alternation of repulsion from, and attraction to, the same object. (Kant 115)

The sublime is like an itch: it feels good, but only insofar as it feels bad. If beauty is pleasure without interest then the sublime is terror without actual threat—it is the feeling of frustration we experience in the presence of something we want to measure but cannot. There are thus two moments of the sublime, dread and awe. These account for Peter's nearly simultaneous love and hatred for Miriam, and the sublime is the confusion that results from the virtual simultaneity of these opposing moments.[18]

Miriam is sublime according to the Kantian definition as well as the colloquial notion with which James would have been familiar. As art she is an image of the ideal, coming alive in a way that the others, even the striking Julia Dallow, do not, but as life she is plain. If Miriam Rooth were to be considered beautiful, then, one would have to conclude that in Kantian terms her beauty is artistic beauty and not natural beauty—according to Kant,

> "A natural beauty is a *beautiful thing*; artistic beauty is a *beautiful presentation* of a thing. . . . Fine art shows its superiority precisely in this, that it describes things beautifully that in nature we would dislike or find ugly" (Kant 179-80).[19]

In the final analysis I accept this distinction: as the novel draws to an end we see Miriam reveling in this artistic beauty. But this beauty is something that she acquires over time. Peter Sherringham's reactions to her throughout the novel show that he is responding to something quite different from beauty. Though Peter thinks she is beautiful and tries to make her so he despises her at the same time that he loves her, and to an equal degree. Miriam knows this and confronts Peter with it repeatedly:

> "How you hate us! Yes, at bottom, below your little taste, you *hate* us!" she repeated. (*TM* 280)

Peter does not hate Miriam, but he hates her profession as much as he loves her person: "It doesn't seem exactly the right sort of thing, young girls meeting actresses" he confides to Nick (*TM* 501), as if young girls and actresses comprised mutually exclusive categories. But they are not mutually exclusive. Since it is impossible to separate Miriam Rooth from her profession we must conclude that Peter both loves her and hates her at the same time.

Peter wants to love Miriam as an object of beauty but he cannot because her profession, her art, repels him—she has the same "brute sublimity" that James maligned Walt Whitman for having twenty-five years before (*LC* 633).[20] Others are similarly both impressed and repelled by her. Julia Dallow says of Miriam:

> "Ah, I dare say it's extremely fine, but I don't care for tragedy when it treads on one's toes. She's like a cow who has kicked over the milking pail. She ought to be tied up!" (*TM* 117)

Peter, though he adores her, will not go so far as to say that she is "fine," calling her instead both "interesting," and "awful" (*TM* 117), (she is later both "extraordinary" and "horrid" [*TM* 166]) and doing so with irritation, thus exhibiting the symptoms of the sublime. At Peter's party for Miriam early on in the novel he finds her performance "indecent" and worries "how he could get her to leave off" (*TM* 114), but his impatience with her recital seems to heighten his enthusiasm for her person:

> He inwardly groaned at the precipitancy with which he had saddled himself with the Tragic Muse (a tragic muse who was noisy and pert), and yet he wished his visitors would go away and leave him alone with her. (*TM* 118)

Though Miriam has neither the "freshness" of Notre Dame nor the purity of Julia she still somehow captivates all those around her, especially Peter Sherringham. Miriam Rooth, like the others, is presented as a work of art, but if she is the new Our Lady, "the great modern personage" (*TM* 315), she is a work of a much different art form than that of the old cathedral. Miriam is not worldly, nor is she wholly an artistic creation, and the traditional categories of art and life thus cannot contain her. Miriam is Notre Dame come alive—she is a work of sublime modernism[21] and Peter's need to see her as beautiful and to try to force her to be beautiful, as if she were a statue, is an error that is both ethical and aesthetical.

The relevance of the Kantian sublime to Miriam Rooth and to the problem of interpreting *The Tragic Muse* is clear. Miriam's magical "effect" is that she evokes the feeling of the sublime in all who see her; when Biddy first sees Miriam she is struck not by her beauty but by the "largely-gazing eyes" that attract her "slightly agitated perception" (*TM* 23). Sherringham, too, is "agitated by her presence" (*TM* 496), becoming more and more confused with her as the story progresses because he is simultaneously infatuated with and repelled by Miriam: "her character was simply to hold you by a particular spell" (*TM* 378) like the "vulgar ghostly vibration" he feels while waiting for Miriam the night of their meeting after the show (*TM* 537). "One side of him is perpetually fighting against the other side," Miriam explains to Nick (*TM* 523). His confusion takes the form of a spell, and this is why Sherringham finds her so disturbing. Peter's anxiety comes from Miriam herself—he has no control over it, and because he is in love with Miriam it can never become anger or hatred for anyone but himself. Yet he continues to find more ways to love Miriam and to make himself more miserable:

> This exasperation, however, was a kind of flattery; it was neither indifference nor simple contempt; it acknowledged a mystifying reality in the girl and even a degree of importance. (*TM* 154)

What Peter feels is neither his own love nor his own hatred, but Miriam's power:

> He guessed that the girl was perfectly prepared to be abused and that her indifference to what might be thought of her discretion was a proof of life, health and spirit, the insolence of conscious power. (*TM* 152)

The simultaneous love and hatred are his feelings but they come from Miriam, and he seems to have no control over them. Sherringham, more than any of the others in the novel, is aware of the power that Miriam possesses—one of the most profound ironies of the book is that he, who is most confused about Miriam and most deluded in his appreciation of her, is the one who shows us the most about her. What he shows us—his primary role in James's design is to show us this—is that Miriam represents a new art form; her "life," her "health" and her "power" are her art. In his confusion he is a foil to Miriam's purity, consistency and power; he illustrates her sublimity. His role in the novel is to measure this power, which is such that the narrator can only describe the effect of it, but though he feels it he cannot comprehend it. This failure is his downfall.

It is a characteristic of actresses in *The Tragic Muse* to evoke the feeling of the sublime in their audiences; even Miriam herself feels the sublime, most notably when she meets Mademoiselle Voisin:

> "Imagine—when she's so perfect!" the girl exclaimed, thoughtfully. "Ah, she kept me off—she kept me off! Her charming manner is in itself a kind of contempt. It's an abyss—it's the wall of China. She has a hard polish, an inimitable surface, like some wonderful porcelain that costs more than you'd think." (*TM* 288)

Mademoiselle Voisin's "charming . . . contempt" is "perfect" and this confusing but compelling perfection, which makes it impossible to view her with disinterest, is sublime. Miriam chooses the hugest and the most perfect images she can think of to describe her impression of the actress but she cannot find the words. The effect of this histrionic sublimity is compounded when Sherringham tries to propose to her in front of the "cold portrait of Rachel" (*TM* 287), the great French actress with whom "his companion suffered little by the juxtaposition" (*TM* 281). Miriam knows the "effect" she has on people, but it takes an ironist like Gabriel Nash to interpret it correctly:

> ... she asked [Nick] if it disgusted him to hear her speak like that, as if she were always posing and thinking about herself, living only to be looked at, thrusting forward her person. She often got sick of doing so, already; but *à la guerre comme à la guerre.*
>
> "That's the fine artistic nature, you see—a sort of divine disgust breaking out in her," Nash expounded. (*TM* 318)

Miriam Rooth, like Mademoiselle Voisin and like Rachel before her, makes her living on her "divine disgust," on the endless paradox of her person that continues to plague Peter Sherringham until the end when he flees to Central America to escape it.[22]

Gabriel Nash, again and again, is the only one who can enjoy this new sublime art—he even uses the term to describe her:

> ... Nash went a step further and regarded her, irresponsibly and sublimely, as a priestess of harmony, with whom the vulgar ideas of success and failure had nothing to do. He laughed at her "parts," holding that without them she would be great. Sherringham envied him his power to content himself with the pleasures he could get: he had a shrewd impression that contentment was not destined to be the sweetener of his own repast. (*TM* 399-400)

Nash's use of the word "sublime" here probably does not indicate the feeling that Kant attempts to rigorously define in the third *Critique*, but his ability to appreciate Miriam's sublimity, his "power to content himself" with the sublime is related to Miriam's power to inspire it. For Nash, Miriam's art is a positive force, but it has the effect of making Peter gradually give up more and more of the things that are important to him—he has by this point given up hope of ever even being happy.

Peter, as I have shown, is confused from beginning to end about Miriam, finding her irresistible and vulgar at the same time. He requires beauty for his peace of mind, and beauty for him seems to entail representation: "I am fond of representation—the representation of life: I like it better, I think, than the real thing" (*TM* 66). The only time Peter is not confused by her presence, in fact, is when he sees Nick's first painting of her. His confusion comes from the "conflict between art and 'the world'" that James mentions in the Preface, a conflict that Miriam transcends in her progression from fiction to realism. It is not surprising, then, that in the context of a conflict between categories—art and the world, beauty and the sublime—the frame between them should prove to be of primary importance.

Nick's first painting of Miriam is unveiled in Chapter 29, one of the most tense chapters in the novel. Peter has come to Nick's studio and has found not Nick Dormer himself but Nick's sister Biddy, who is in love with him and who is hard at work on a clay bust of her brother. Peter is preoccupied in the scene with being magnanimous and showing "how much he liked [Biddy] in order to make her forgive him for not liking her more" (*TM* 361), and she herself is upset about the recent failure of her brother's engagement to Julia and about what Nick's behavior has done to their mother. The painting itself, of course, which is responsible for Julia's decision to give Nick up (though she has never seen it), is "in the room, put away with its face to the wall" (*TM* 373). It is in this scene, too, that Peter learns from Biddy of Nick's plans to "chuck" his seat in the House of Commons[23] (*TM* 371), and he is stunned by this news:

> To learn that there was something for which he was ready to renounce such honours, and to recognize the nature of that bribe, affected Sherringham powerfully and strangely. He felt as if he had heard the sudden blare of a trumpet, and he felt at the same time as if he had received a sudden slap in the face. Nick's bribe was "art"—the strange temptress with whom he himself had been wrestling and over whom he had finally ventured to believe that wisdom and training had won a victory. (*TM* 372)

Peter's own infatuation with the "strange temptress" of art is rekindled when he hears the news. He feels immediately once again the simultaneous dread/awe of the sublime and becomes as anxious about the painting as Biddy has shown herself to be.

I make the obvious identification here between this "strange temptress" and Miriam herself, the "priestess of art" and "incarnation of beauty" (*TM* 396), because the image it conjures is crucial to my reading of the novel. James also employs it in his "Introduction to *The Tempest*" (1907), where he finds in Shakespeare's play "the instant sense of some copious equivalent of thought for every grain of the grossness of reality" in it (*LC* 1207). Shakespeare's last play is thus "the rarest of all examples of literary art" (*LC* 1208) because it is completely and perfectly designed—it is artistic, devoid of what he calls "arbitrary marks" (*LC* 1217). The deliberateness of the play has long caused readers to wonder whether *The Tempest* was Shakespeare's "farewell to the stage," but James encourages readers of Shakespeare's play to forego this question, and with it the "affirmed conclusions, complacencies of conviction, full apprehensions of the meaning and triumphant pointings of the moral" (*LC* 1205) that critics have offered in answer to it. Instead, James instructs us to appreciate the calm perfection of the play, which he compares to both the eye of a storm and the statue of a god in a single telling metaphor:

> to approach the general bone of contention, as we can but familiarly name it, for whatever purpose, we have to cross the scene of action at a mortal risk, making the fewest steps of it and trusting to the probable calm at the centre of the storm. There in fact, though there only, we find that serenity; find the subject itself intact and unconscious, seated as unwinking and inscrutable as a divinity in a temple, save for that vague flicker of derision, the only response to our interpretive heat, which adds the last beauty to its face. The divinity never relents—never, like the image in The Winter's Tale, steps down from its pedestal; it simply leaves us to stare on through the ages, with this fact indeed of having crossed the circle of fire, and so got into the real and right relation to it, for our one comfort. (*LC* 1205-06)

James describes the play, "a divinity in a temple," in much the same terms as those he uses to characterize Miriam Rooth, a "priestess of art" on a pedestal. *The Tempest* is thus a statue that sits at the center of the storm of history and commentary—it "never steps down from its pedestal"; it never, that is, gives us any answers to the questions it raises because it is pure art. It is wrought not by "experience" but by "expression" (*LC* 1211) and bears no direct connection to "the grossness of reality."

This statuary imagery, as we have seen, is one that is used constantly in *The Tragic Muse*, and it is used most often and most poignantly to describe Miriam herself:

> the cold passion of art had perched on her banner . . . she seemed now like the finished statue lifted from the ground to its pedestal. (*TM* 261)

Later Miriam admires the peaceful conditions of the portrait painter—"He was quiet, independent, absolute, free to do what he liked as he liked it, shut up in his little temple with his altar and his divinity" (*TM* 514)—but she can never become such an artist because she is the divinity itself. Nick Dormer's first painting of this modern Melpomene, like Shakespeare's *Tempest*, is so impressive because it is so perfectly artistic. Sherringham's first view of the painting, and ours as well, is a startling and mystical experience:

> Unfinished, simplified and in some portions merely suggested, it was strong, brilliant and vivid and had already the look of life and the air of an original thing . . . Miriam was represented in three-quarters, seated, almost down to her feet. She leaned forward, with one of her legs crossed over the other, her

arms extended and foreshortened, her hands locked together around her knee. (*TM* 375)

This painting of Miriam, like the novel, is a representation both of a representation and of representation itself. As an actress, a follower of other people's scripts, Miriam has been placed upon a pedestal by her profession and especially by Peter Sherringham, who wants to make her an art object. The painting portrays Miriam not as a real woman but as a work of art—the face is "painted" and the arms are "moulded" (*TM* 376, 375), and we, through Peter Sherringham, are conscious that this is an image, a representation of one artist by another:

> Her beautiful head was bent a little, broodingly, and her splendid face seemed to look down at life. She had a grand appearance of being raised aloft, with a wide regard, from a height of intelligence, for the great field of the artist, all the figures and passions he may represent. (*TM* 375)

Miriam, with "her expression of gloomy grandeur" (*TM* 515), is "*bête*" in life but beautiful in art. In the painting she appears "raised aloft," radiating artistic genius and "æsthetic passion" like Shakespeare's last romance (*LC* 1209). Like *The Tempest* she seems to stay on her pedestal—she is poetic, not realistic, in Nick's first triumphant rendering of her. As Peter walks through London the next day his mind is full of the glory of the theater:

> . . . he saw comedy and drama and passion and character and English life; he saw all humanity and history and poetry, and perpetually, in the midst of them, shining out in the high relief of some great moment, an image as fresh as an unveiled statue. (*TM* 379)

As "unwinking and inscrutable" as Shakespeare's play, she has in the painting all the Kantian beauty that Peter Sherringham wants to see in her, and he reacts to her portrait the same way that Nick reacts to Notre Dame. The painting has precisely the freshness of "an unveiled statue" to him: he gazes at Miriam's "beautiful head" and leaves the studio with "a quickened rush, a sense of the beauty of Miriam" (*TM* 376). Mrs Rooth, also, is later struck by the beauty of the thing:

> "It *is* serious, it *is* grand," murmured Mrs Rooth, who had taken up a rapt attitude before the portrait of her daughter. "It makes one wonder what she's thinking of. Beautiful, commendable things—that's what it seems to say." (*TM* 516)[24]

But this dynamic scene in Nick's studio is more than a reminder of Nick's talent and Miriam's beauty (which, as we have seen, does not exist in life). The complexity and subtlety of the scene have less to do with the painting itself than with the way it is presented. Peter does not view the painting as it is, unfinished and unframed in the corner of Nick's studio. Instead, Biddy holds it for him, in essence framing the painting herself:

> She wouldn't let him take it; she bade him stand off and allow her to place it in the right position. In this position she carefully presented it, supporting it, at the proper angle, from behind and showing her head and shoulders above it. (*TM* 374-75)

The contiguity of images here is hilariously complicated. Miriam is "raised aloft" "in the right position" for the edification of Peter, who is in love with her, by Biddy, who is in love with Peter. Like a frame, Biddy herself cannot even see the painting she is presenting:

> Biddy Dormer abstained from looking round the corner of the canvas as she held it; she only watched, in Peter's eyes, for *his* impression of it. (*TM* 375)

"Poor Biddy" supports the unfinished painting "from behind," "at the proper angle," acting as a frame for the frameless painting and heightening the effect of Miriam's looking down on the world from her pedestal. Biddy thus becomes Miriam's pedestal. But at the same time Biddy herself is also in a manner framed by the painting, "showing her [own] head and shoulders above it." In this poignantly visual scene we see Biddy Dormer as if she were a bust, a clay sculptured head, supported for a moment by the painting as if by a pedestal. The effect of this scene is a violent tension equal to that in *The Turn of the Screw* when the Governess after seeing Quint framed by the window immediately runs outside to investigate, only to become a similar image in the same window, scaring Mrs. Grose.[25] The image of Miriam's fine "brooding" head vying with Biddy's for primacy places the two in competition—one must be the work, the other the parergon or frame—and asks the now tantalizing question of which of the women Peter will eventually marry.[26]

This scene blurs more forcefully than any other scene in the novel the distinction between art and life, and this obfuscation is accomplished via the frame that traditionally separates them. The scene shows Miriam's artificial image, which is always difficult to distinguish ontologically from Miriam herself, straining for primacy over her environment and forcing "poor Biddy" into a subordinate role. Miriam appears here ready to burst out of her role as image, object and Muse and to forge her own identity while Biddy fades into the background.

Miriam appears here in a vague and puzzling state: she is an art work, one that is not even finished, yet she seems in effect to be alive and present. She has, in fact, been in this ambiguous state for some time when Nick first paints her portrait. Her profession is a public one but her status among the public, and especially with Peter, is far from clear. His conversations with Miriam expose his inability to see her in more complex terms than those of the binary conflict between art and life:

> "What's rare in you is that you have—as I suspect, at least—no nature of your own." Miriam listened to this as if she were preparing to argue or not, only as it should strike her as being a pleasing picture; but as yet, naturally, she failed to understand. "You are always playing something; there are no intervals. It's the absence of intervals, of a *fond* or background, that I don't comprehend. You're an embroidery without a canvas." (*TM* 167)

Miriam has neither the "nature" of life nor the "*fond*" of art: while the Dormer family, at the start of the story, is "unaddicted to enriching any bareness of contact with verbal or any other embroidery" Peter sees Miriam here as "an embroidery without a canvas," which is much the same as calling her a bust without a pedestal. If the Grace and Lady Agnes are canvas without paint Miriam is a painted image without a canvas or background—she is art with nothing to separate her from life. Miriam's perfection and her unrelenting style are her art; they are her profession, and they produce the "effect" that is her art. But Peter is confused because she has no "intervals" or "background." Art, he seems to reason, must have a background, but Miriam, even as an image, has no background but life itself.

Peter constantly changes his mind about the question of her character as well as about her status as an art object. At one point she has "no countenance of her own, but only the countenance of the occasion, a sequence, a variety (capable possibly of becoming immense), of representative movements" (TM 151); at another, after viewing Nick's painting of her, she seems to have the complete pervasive presence that Gabriel Nash has:

> The idea of her having no character of her own came back to him with a force that made him laugh in the empty street: this was a disadvantage she was so exempt from that he appeared to himself not to have known her till to-night. (*TM* 378)

Here he changes his mind about her, seeing her now not as life but as art. As I have shown, the painting relieves, if only temporarily, the torment of his confusion:

> He floated in a sense of the felicity of it, in the general encouragement of a thing perfectly done, in the almost aggressive bravery of still larger claims for an art which could so triumphantly, so exquisitely render life. "Render it?" Peter said to himself. "Create it and reveal it, rather; give us something new and large and of the first order!" (*TM* 378)

The root of Peter's confusion has been his need to frame Miriam, and the emergence of the painting, in which all the world is her "superior, glorious stage," brings him a catharsis of sorts. She is here an actual work of art, framed by life and as "encaged and provided for" within this frame as Lambert Strether is described as being in the Preface to *The Ambassadors* (*TA* 11). To Peter Sherringham this represents the culmination of her evolution, but I think it clearly shows that her development toward complete realism, the fusion of image and life, has only just begun.

As James wrote in the Preface to *The Awkward Age*, in the passage with which I begin the present work,

> though the relations of a human figure or a social occurrence are what make such objects interesting, they also make them, to the same tune, difficult to isolate, to surround with the sharp black line, to frame in the square, the circle, the charming oval, that helps any arrangement of objects to become a picture. (*AA* 5)

Miriam Rooth is precisely difficult to frame; this, perhaps, is why Nick never finishes the painting. She transcends the frame in life as well as in art, always wishing to be on her own, to be able to act alone as the painter does: "'Oh, I hate scenery!' sighed Miriam" (*TM* 268). The scenery that adorns her performances, it is true, is her background or frame, and though she makes it clear that her wish is to be free of it she appears bound by a frame in life if not in art. She depends upon her public: "We are your tables and chairs, the simple furniture of your life" (*TM* 280) Peter Sherringham insists, and Nash seems to agree:

> "She has great courage, but should you speak of her as solitary, with such a lot of us all round her?" Gabriel asked. (*TM* 439)

But the frame that separates her from life is obscured by the fact that she is neither a mere *femme du monde* nor a statue but an actress, and as such she is able to work both within the frame and outside of its confines:

> As soon as she stepped on the boards a great and special alteration usually took place in her—she was in focus and in her frame; yet there were hours too in which she wore her world's face before the audience, just as there were hours too in which she wore her stage face in the world. She took up either mask as it suited her humour. To-day Sherringham was seeing each in its order, and he thought each the best. (*TM* 476)

It is this continual switching back and forth between art and life that makes Miriam sublime, both in art and in life. It causes Peter's infatuation/repulsion—Miriam always presents the infinite in the finite.

She wears the mask of her art and the mask of her life, and the frame is thus not a cage that contains her but a mask, a tool of her trade.

There are two ways in which Miriam could free herself from the bonds of the frames that contain her. One of these, to simply leave the stage and join the horde, to relinquish her magic like Prospero and "descend; be stone no more" like Hermione[27]—to simply renounce one world for another—is not an option for her. She must find life within the bounds of art—she must bring life to the stage. In the end of *The Tragic Muse* Miriam is a finished product of sublime literary realism, not the art of sculpture. Her character is complete not when she is framed or lifted to her pedestal but when she has brought life within its bounds. Miriam keeps her tragic mask, making no attempt to renounce it as Nick renounces his political one, and her ability to do this is an indication of her greater strength. She accepts categorization as actress and Muse but demands also the right to transcend this frame, and she blossoms within its confines.

Nick Dormer's first painting of Miriam, for all the complexities of its presentation, is poetical and artificial, but his second painting is to be "as different as possible from that thing" (*TM* 495):

> "What I ought to do is to try something as different as possible from that thing; not the sibyl, the muse, the tremendous creature, but the charming woman, the person one knows, in different gear, as she appears *en ville*, as she calls it." (*TM* 495)

This second painting is to be a realistic one that will portray Miriam not as an artistic muse but as a woman, and Miriam looks forward to the simplicity of the realism she and Nick have worked so hard to accomplish:

> "We're washing our dirty linen before you, but it's all right," Miriam answered, "because it shows you what sort of people we are, and that's what you need to know. Don't make me vague and arranged and fine, in this new thing," she continued: "make me characteristic and real; make life, with all its horrid facts and truths, stick out of me. I wish you could put mother in too; make us live there side by side and tell our little story. 'The wonderful actress and her still more wonderful mamma'—don't you think that's an awfully good subject?" (*TM* 526)

"This new thing" will make Miriam live. It will be hardly a thing at all—it will be a work that will attempt to somehow transcend its own thingness. Biddy's "shapeless mass," which "was intended, or would be intended after a while, for Nick" (*TM* 361), is a thing, as is Nick's first painting, though the two can hardly be compared, but "this new thing" will be a life, an event. It will portray the "mystifying reality" of her character, and her character is simply her unremitting honesty:

> "You're an embroidery without a canvas."
> "Yes, perhaps," the girl replied, with her head on one side, as if she were looking at the pattern. "But I'm very honest." (*TM* 167)

Honesty is Miriam's approach to her art and her solution to the problem of Sherringham's infatuation with her: "I represent, but I represent truly" (*TM* 528).[28]

This honesty will be both the subject and the object of Nick's second painting, through which Miriam will attempt to build a new category for herself and emerge as a masterpiece of sublime modernist realism:

> I want to do the modern too. I want to do *le drame,* with realistic effects. (*TM* 269)

As both subject and object, her honesty will unite her art with Nick's, thus realizing the "mighty pictorial fusion" (*AN* 84) of art and life that James describes in the Preface:

> My business was accordingly to "go in" for complete pictorial fusion, some such common interest between my first two notions as would, in spite of their birth under quite different stars, do them no violence at all. (*AN* 84-85)

Miriam, like Gabriel Nash, is fusing her art with her life—she has made her life a work of art and her art a work of life. When she sits for Nick the second time her pedestal disappears, and she has no more need of a frame. She performs even as she sits:

> "I like to hear you talk—it makes you live, brings you out," Nick mentioned. "And you sit beautifully still." (*TM* 526)

> Miriam's account of her mother's views was a scene of comedy, and there was instinctive art in the way she added touch to touch and made point upon point. She was so quiet, to oblige her painter, that only her fine lips moved—all her expression was in her charming utterance. (*TM* 528)

Two things are happening simultaneously here. As she gives the account of her mother's views, Miriam is an artist—she is artful, and her words are beautiful. Though she is performing, however, she is not acting but simply telling the truth. Nick's painting, then, to couch it in literary terms, will be a work not of fiction but of realism. Miriam has become realism incarnate. Nick's painting will be successful because of Miriam's realism and his own sensitivity to it. Thus a representation of an actress, a dissembler who has been thought by some to have no character of her own at all, is still somehow real. Peter's failure to grasp this reality condemns him to exile, and Nick's understanding of it makes him an artist.

This second painting is not so much a painting as a dynamic event. Miriam's realism makes, as she claims, a perfect subject for Nick, but his painting provides her with both peace—"*This* is the peace I want!" (*TM* 530)—and a chance to represent herself truly, a chance she has long been wanting. Nick and Miriam are attempting to do the same thing at the same time, and each succeeds because of the other. Nick must paint Miriam, the muse through whom he has finally been able to become an artist, and Miriam finds in sitting for Nick the same purifying satisfaction that Peter had hoped she would produce in her audience:

> "It rests me, this little devoted corner; oh, it rests me. It's out of the tussle and the heat, it's deliciously still, and they can't get at me. Ah, when art's like this, *à la bonne heure!*" (*TM* 514-15)

Miriam comes to Nick's studio to escape "the vulgarities of the day" (*TM* 269) as others come to her, thus bridging the gap both between subject and object and between art and life.

Miriam also bridges the abyss between beauty and the sublime, transcending even the frame between these mutually exclusive categories. This is the goal of all sublime art. She is still an actress, a heroine of representation, in the end of the novel, and her performance the night of her "*première*" (*TM* 499) is stellar:

> She was beauty, she was music, she was truth; she was passion and persuasion and tenderness. She caught up the obstreperous play in soothing, entwining arms and carried it into the high places of poetry, of style. And she had such tones of nature, such concealments of art, such effusions of life, that the whole scene glowed with the colour she communicated, and the house, as if pervaded by rosy fire, glowed back at the scene. (*TM* 531)

Miriam, though she is not herself beautiful, is beauty itself on the stage—she is "transmuted" now more than ever before from the actual to the ideal, and her beauty now is not in presentation or representation but in their happy combination in her performance. But her "performance [is] a living thing, with a power to change, to grow, to develop, to beget new forms of the same life" (*TM* 391), and she is also sublime:

> [Peter's] state of mind was of the strangest and he was conscious of its strangeness, just as he was conscious in his very person of a cessation of resistance which likened itself absurdly to liberation. He felt weak at the same time that he felt inspired, and he felt inspired at the same time that he knew, or believed he knew, that his face was a blank. He saw things as a shining confusion, and yet somehow something monstrously definite kept surging out

of them. Miriam was a beautiful, actual, fictive, impossible young woman, of a past age, an undiscoverable country, who spoke in blank verse and overflowed with metaphor, who was exalted and heroic beyond all human convenience, and who yet was irresistibly real and related to one's own affairs.

(*TM* 533-34)

Miriam's state of perfect presence throws Peter Sherringham into "a shining confusion": she is "actual" and yet "impossible" and "fictive" and yet "irresistibly real," "exalted and heroic" and yet "monstrously definite"—in short, she is both of this world and of another, as evidenced by the allusion to Hamlet's "To be or not to be" soliloquy.[29] We submit to the pressures of our lives, Prince Hamlet reasons, because we have no assurance that what follows in the "undiscovered country" will not be worse than what we now suffer. Hamlet fears the realm of death, but Peter Sherringham's fear, Miriam's "undiscoverable country," is that of life. Like the Danish prince, Peter is not yet ready to venture to this far away place.

The fact that Peter Sherringham's confusion is intensified instead of pacified by this increase in Miriam's perfection is puzzling, but the reason for it, which should be clear by now, is that hers, though she is described here as "beautiful," is a sublime perfection like that of Mademoiselle Voisin and not a beautiful one. According to Kant, of course, a work of art cannot be sublime because the sublime involves magnitudes too vast for most art works to encompass.[30] The sublime, as a contrapurposive feeling, is not ordinarily compatible with beauty, but Kant does consider the possibility of sublime art in a situation in which two arts are combined:

the exhibition of the sublime may, insofar as it belongs to fine art, be combined with beauty in a *tragedy in verse*, in a *didactic poem*, or in an *oratorio*; and in these combinations fine art is even more artistic. But whether it is also more beautiful (given how great a variety of different kinds of liking cross one another) may in some cases be doubted. (Kant 195)

Such art can be sublime because it represents two art forms, and thus two "kinds of liking," in a single object, and this is certainly the case with Miriam Rooth. In Kant's example of the tragic poem, if one apprehends the poetic element of the work the tragedy seems infinite while if one considers the tragedy of the plot the fact that such a tragedy is expressed in verse is vast and confusing—"this time she had verse to deal with" the narrator recalls with admiration (TM 531). This fusion of two art forms in one is clearly an aspect of drama and also one of the art of portraiture, as

Nick makes clear in his conversation with Nash in their box in the theater:

> He insisted, above all, on the interest, the richness arising from this great peculiarity of [portraiture]: that, unlike most other forms, it was a revelation of two realities, the man whom it was the artist's conscious effort to reveal and the man (the interpreter) expressed in the very quality and temper of that effort. It offered a double vision, the strongest dose of life that art could give, the strongest dose of art that life could give. (*TM* 328)

Nick views Miriam's perfectly sublime performance with "interest," admiring not the beauty but the "peculiarity" of it, and this peculiarity inspires him to contemplate the art of portraiture. Nick Dormer's second painting will capture this peculiar sublimity. It will be a combinatory work like those Kant mentions as sublime because it is a pictorial representation of an actress: the painter's art will be fused with that of his objective subject.[31] The scene, likewise, is a dramatization of a pictorial work in progress.

As Derrida notes in *The Truth in Painting*, "There cannot, it seems, be a *parergon* for the sublime" (*TP* 127). Since the sublime cannot be framed, it is as fitting as it is frustrating that the second painting is not only never finished but never even seen in the novel. The painting remains a process, an event, and one that is dramatized rather than described. It is a fusion of painting and drama unencumbered by thingness or objecthood—the painting is thus simply the end of the novel itself. The portrait becomes the novel. Life becomes art and art becomes life, and the result of this life-within-art-within-life—all within the confines of a novel—is not fiction but literary realism. In the end Miriam is a masterpiece not of theater or even of painting, but of story.

The answer to the question of what Henry James has done "about art" lies in Miriam Rooth's sublimity—he has accomplished the production of sublimity in art. There are two ways that one could experience the "undiscovered country" that Hamlet mentions and to which Peter Sherringham alludes, and each way involves a fusion of art and life in which the frame between them is dissolved. One way is to follow Gabriel Nash in renouncing the material world and living only in the realm of beauty. But as we have seen, to do this is simply to disappear, to become a ghost, as both Nash and Peter Sherringham do in the end of the novel: Nash "melt[s] back into the elements" (*TM* 602) "for all the world as in some Hawthorn tale" (*TM* 597) and Peter flees to the equator. The other way is what I have called realism, the fusion of art and life that James mentions in the Preface to the novel.

While Miriam is constructing new aesthetic categories for herself Peter Sherringham is being slowly and painfully deconstructed. Sherringham's problem, his tragic flaw, as it were, is that he doesn't see the relationship between art and life that James puts forward in Miriam Rooth, insisting on a hierarchy in which life has precedence over art. He offers Miriam the chance to follow him out of her own world, the world of "fables," and into his:

> "The stage is great, no doubt, but the world is greater. It's bigger than any of those places in the Strand. We'll go in for realities instead of fables, and you'll do them far better than you do the fables." (*TM* 543)

Peter, who refuses to sacrifice life to art, requires that Miriam sacrifice art for life, but his supplications bounce back at him: "Stay on *my* stage; come off your own," she later implores him for the sake of argument (*TM* 545). Even then Sherringham persists:

> "Would *you* accept them, from me?—accept the sacrifice, see me throw up my work, my prospects (of course I should have to do that), and simply become your appendage?"
>
> "My dear fellow, you invite me with the best conscience in the world to become yours."
>
> "The cases are not equal." (*TM* 546)

They are equal, of course, and Sherringham's division of the world into "realities" and "fables" is a false division: the frame between them is now itself a fable. In *The Tragic Muse* life is to be lived not instead of art but through it. Sherringham's downfall is thus a result of more than his selfishness: it is a result of a serious aesthetic flaw in his understanding of the world. "A creature who is *all* an artist—I am curious to see that" (*TM* 168), Peter ejaculates early on in the story, but he has continually seen such an artist, and he has failed to understand her.

The best joke of the novel, of course, is that Nick's second painting of Miriam Rooth, the realistic, living one, will be sent when it is finished to Peter Sherringham, the great aesthete, and his new wife Biddy, ever "a devoted Electra, laying a cool, healing hand on a distracted Orestes" (*TM* 498). The painting will adorn their new life together in the jungles of an unnamed and perhaps better-left-undiscovered country near the equator, and we may well shake our heads and murmur with Miriam: "'Poor Sherringham—with *that!*'" (*TM* 586).

CHAPTER II

The Turn of the Screw: Exquisite Mystification, Pure Romance

> I do not know what is essential and what is accessory in a work. And above all I do not know what this thing is, that is neither essential nor accessory, neither proper nor improper, and that Kant calls *parergon*, for example the frame. Where does the frame take place. Does it take place. Where does it begin. Where does it end. What is its internal limit. Its external limit. And its surface between the two limits.
>
> Jacques Derrida, *Parergon*[1]

Interest in the frame as a structural element in James's fiction has focused mainly on *The Turn of the Screw*, the only one of his major works that is explicitly framed, and it is this to which I now turn. Alexander E. Jones writes that the frame of the tale, the dramatization of Douglas's telling of it, is simply a typical "parenthetical device" used to make the reader "suspend his broad-daylight common-sense disbelief and enter the mood of the story" (Jones 112), but this view has been much questioned in recent decades by critics who read the Prologue as an incomplete or broken frame.[2] Susan Crowl rejects Jones's view of the Prologue as what she calls a "detachable stereotype" (Crowl 111) and reads the frame as being intimately connected to the story but incomplete and problematic, calling it "a half-frame which is full of suggestive, if veiled, commentary on the story to follow" (Crowl 108):

> In my view, the form is left unfinished in this way in order to leave unfinished to our judgement the questions which occur in turn to the governess, to Douglas, and to James. (Crowl 110)

Crowl argues that the form of the novella is echoed ironically by the "double frame and subtle shifting of identity" in the story itself (Crowl 114): "The form of the story, an introductory frame and tale within a tale, is similarly consistent and repetitive in the nested inversions of reality and story-book romance which are the governess' attempt at a perspective on her shifting experiences at Bly" (Crowl 122).

William Goetz takes much the same position. In "The 'Frame' of *The Turn of the Screw*: Framing the Reader In," Goetz discusses the Prologue to the tale, "an exemplary scene by which James tells us how to read the tale" (Goetz 71), and its function as a framing device. He concludes that "the 'frame' of *The Turn of the Screw* is asymmetrical" (Goetz 73): we expect an epilogue, Goetz claims, that will explain the text that the Prologue has introduced, a completion of the frame, but "The 'frame' shows us through its incompleteness that there is no easy recourse to an author, whether implied or real, just as for the governess herself there is to be no recourse to the Master" (Goetz 73). Goetz's notion of the incompleteness of the frame is echoed more recently by Richard Rust in an article on thresholds in the novella:

> We try to control our lives and prevent the terror of the liminal by providing frames or by confronting our fears.
>
> . . . Yet the story ends terribly unframed with the shocking death of Miles. The horror is accentuated by the undermining of the frame structure itself, something we counted on to provide control. (Rust 444)

In short, there seems to be a recent critical consensus that *The Turn of the Screw* is only partially framed and that the incompleteness of the frame is somehow necessary, or at least appropriate, as a compliment to the incompleteness of the governess's narrative itself.

My feeling is that while critics are right to stress the connectedness and appropriateness of the frame to the story they are wrong to argue that the frame is incomplete. Previous readings of the Prologue to *The Turn of the Screw* have been limited by their dependence on a static and simplistic notion of framing that relies too heavily on comparison with the rectangular frame of a painting. I will argue here that the Prologue, or frame, and the story itself are not simply juxtaposed, like a broken frame around a broken painting. The tightness of the story alone—what James called the "small strength," "unattackable ease," and "perfect homogeneity" of the tale—would seem to indicate a flaw in the half-frame theory. The Prologue is not a broken frame at all but a complete one that describes events occurring both before and after the story,[3] thus framing the manuscript temporally and providing the closure that critics argue is missing. There is little basis for the claim that the story should be further framed by an epilogue that would answer the problems of the text. In order to demonstrate and explore the completeness of the frame and its function we require a more sophisticated notion of the concept of frame than has yet been offered, and for this I appeal to Derrida's *The Truth in Painting*. My purpose is to use Derrida's notion of the "*parergon*" to explore the mechanics of the relationship between the Prologue and the tale itself.

Derrida's essay " Parergon" is a philosophical treatment of the frame as a structural constituent. The parergon ("beside-work"), of which the picture frame is merely the most accessible example, is more than just a decorative enclosure of a work. It is that which is not part of the work of art but without which the work cannot exist as a work, like the signature of a drawing, the drapery that necessarily fails to cover the body of a nude woman in a figure painting (without which she would be merely naked), or the columns outside a building. "The parergon," Derrida writes, "is precisely an ill-detachable detachment" (*TP* 59), an entity that both is and cannot be separated from the work:

> A parergon comes against, beside, in addition to the *ergon*, the work done, the fact, the work, but it does not fall to one side, it touches and cooperates with the operation, from a certain outside. Neither simply outside nor simply inside. Like an accessory that one is obliged to welcome on the border, on board. It is first of all the on (the) bo(a)rd(er).[4] (*TP* 54)

Like the Prologue to *The Turn of the Screw*, the parergon, on board but on the border, is of the work but not in the work. It is necessarily both present to and necessarily excluded from the work. It belongs to the work extrinsically and is thus separate both from the work and from that from which it separates the work:

> *Parerga* have a thickness, a surface which separates them not only (as Kant would have it) from the integral inside, from the body proper of the *ergon*, but also from the outside, from the wall on which the painting is hung, from the space in which the statue or column is erected, from the whole field of historical, economic, political inscription in which the drive to signature is produced. (*TP* 61)

Since the parergon separates both the inside from the outside and the outside from the inside, it stands away from both the inside and the outside simultaneously like figure on ground. When it performs its function, however, when it frames, it disappears completely:

> The *parergon* stands out both from the *ergon* (the work) and from the milieu, it stands out first of all like a figure on a ground. . . . But the parergonal frame stands out against two grounds, but with respect to each of these two grounds, it merges into the other. . . . There is always a form on a ground, but the parergon is a form which has as its traditional determination not that it stands

> out, but that it disappears, buries itself, effaces itself, melts away at the moment it deploys its greatest energy. (*TP* 61)

The parergonal frame, then, blurs into the exterior when the focus is on the interior, and it blurs into the interior, accentuating the work, when the focus is on the exterior.[5] This is clearly illustrated by *The Turn of the Screw*—at the beginning the Prologue appears part of the novel but by the end we have completely forgotten that we are in a room full of people by a fire. The Prologue first jumps forward and forces both figure and ground into the background but then fades away, disappearing into the outside when one looks intently at the inside of the work. The frame, in other words, cannot be in the background, and this is the source of its power. The parergon is secondary but it cannot be secondary. Shoshana Felman perhaps has this chameleonic effect of the parergon in mind when she writes that

> The frame [of *The Turn of the Screw*] is therefore not an outside contour whose role is to display an inside content: it is a kind of exteriority which permeates the very heart of the story's interiority, an internal cleft separating the story's content from itself, distancing it from its own referential certainty. With respect to the story's content, the frame thus acts both as an inclusion of the exterior and an exclusion of the interior: it is a perturbation of the outside at the very core of the story's inside, and as such, it is a blurring of the very difference between inside and outside. (Felman 123)

The Prologue exists beside the work, it is separate from both the inside and the outside of the work, and it appears part of the inside if the viewer's focus is on the inside and vice versa.

The most important characteristic of the parergon, however, and the one that will prove most useful to my analysis of James's novels, is that it comes into being, or is necessitated, because of a lacuna, a lack in the work. It derives its paradoxical nature from the work itself, Derrida writes, but from something absent from the work rather than something present to it:

> The *parergon* inscribes something which comes as an extra, *exterior* to the proper field . . . but whose transcendent exteriority comes to play, abut onto, brush against, rub, press the limit itself and intervene in the inside only to the extent that the inside is lacking. It is lacking *in* something and it is lacking *from itself*. (*TP* 56)

The parergon is present because of something in the work itself that is not present. That the parergon clearly lacks the work and cannot stand alone is obvious, but it is less obvious that the work also lacks the frame and that the frame is necessitated by a lack in the work. The relation between the Prologue and the tale in James's *The Turn of the Screw* is similar to the relationship Derrida describes between the painting and the frame. To understand the Prologue, and to show how and why the frame is complete, it is necessary to isolate the lack in James's story that prompted him to complicate it with the addition of a prologue.

The Prologue to *The Turn of the Screw* is called a Prologue by critics because the narrator uses the term, presumably after Douglas himself: "It appeared that the narrative he had promised to read us really required for a proper intelligence a few words of prologue" (*TS* 4). It is necessary to distinguish clearly, however, between the Prologue and what I will call here the 'prologue,' especially since both preface different works entitled "The Turn of the Screw." The Prologue frames the novella, while the 'prologue,' which is contained by the Prologue and part of it, is Douglas's introduction of his manuscript to which the narrator refers. The 'prologue' summarizes not only the conditions of the governess's employment but also the details of the uncle's residence in town and the turn of events through which he has come to be in charge of Miles and Flora (*TS* 4). This 'prologue,' according to Douglas, is necessitated by the audience, who without such an introduction would supposedly have trouble understanding the story. Douglas's 'prologue' has the odd effect of making it unclear to the reader exactly where the story starts; the first sentences of the governess's narrative seem to imply that others once came before them. This 'prologue,' which he deems necessary but which we must simply accept, is not given to us directly, but is rather summarized by the narrator after the fact. The invisible 'prologue,' given to us indirectly, is a hole in the frame, a gap between the Prologue to the novella and the actual manuscript. The 'prologue' is that strange and imperceptible place where the frame overlaps and intertwines with the story proper, where all horizon lines fade into the distance.

But what necessitates the Prologue, the scene by the fire in the country house, in the first place? James added the dramatic Prologue because the governess's narrative is lacking something, and this lack is no mere uncertainty or ambiguity in the text, such as the question of whether or not the ghosts are real or that of whether the governess actually suffocates Miles in the end. An answer to either of these questions would become part of the work and augment it considerably, as James is clearly aware in the Preface to the New York edition of the novella when he writes: "this perfectly independent and irresponsible little fiction rejoices, beyond any rival on a like ground, in a conscious provision of prompt retort to the sharpest question that may be addressed to it" (*TS* 117). The "prompt retort," of course, is that such questions are unanswerable. Deliberate ambiguity, as so many recent critics have pointed out, is a necessary part of the structure of the tale, and James makes clear in his Preface that all the particulars that would resolve the ambiguities of his text are purposefully omitted from his story so that it might not fail as dismally as those of his competitors. He writes in the Preface of some of the other ghost narratives that were currently being published:

> One had seen, in fiction, some grand form of wrong-doing, or better still of wrong-being, imputed, seen it promised and announced as by the hot breath of the Pit—and then, all lamentably, shrink to the compass of some particular brutality, some particular immorality, some particular infamy portrayed: with the result, alas, of the demonstration's falling sadly short.[6] (*TS* 122)

The purpose of the Prologue, then, cannot be to answer to a question asked by the text. The story, however, since it is so obviously framed, must (according to the theory of the parergon) have a more fundamental lack that cannot be eliminated internally, a lack that distinguishes it from the ordinary novel. We find that it does. John Carlos Rowe has argued that "the mise en abyme of the manuscript is an effect of the Uncle and his disguised power" (Rowe 143). More generally, however, I suggest that what the governess's manuscript is missing is simply a beginning. Her narrative simply does not begin, and it cannot: a beginning would violate its form.

One might object, of course, that the governess's story as we have it begins at chapter one—the word 'beginning' is even found in the first line of the governess's narrative:

> I remember the whole beginning as a succession of flights and drops, a little see-saw of the right throbs and the wrong. (*TS* 6)

There is nothing within her narrative, furthermore, that indicates explicitly that it lacks a beginning, but of course if the lack were so explicit, that which satisfied it would be not a frame but an element of the story itself, hence Derrida's paradoxical reminder that "There is no natural frame. *There is* frame, but the frame *does not exist*" (*TP* 81). We learn of the lack not from the work but from the frame itself. Douglas, who knows the story and knew its author, says that the beginning is missing, and the narrator repeats his words: "the written statement took up the tale at a point after it had, in a manner, begun" (*TS* 4). Douglas's 'prologue' is an attempt, embedded within the drama of the frame, to set the scene, to provide "the fact to be in possession of" (*TS* 4). It is this nakedness of the manuscript, this lack of the essential "fact," that the 'prologue' is to expiate to the listeners around the fire. The word "beginning" emphasizes not the beginning itself but the fact that the beginning is absent and must remain so. The Prologue as a whole redresses this lack by replacing the beginning.

The only other hint in the story, once we look for it, of a missing beginning is the past-perfect narration in the first paragraph of the first chapter. There is nothing unique or problematic about pluperfection in the early pages of a novel, of course, but the past-perfect mode is employed specifically to refer to something that came before a given action in the past. There is no indication that pages are missing from the manuscript, or that its author would have liked to pick up the story earlier; the story has a confessional tone, as if the governess, like the narrator of "The Way it Came" (1896),[7] never meant for her story to be read by anyone but herself and, perhaps, Douglas.[8] In most novels, of course, this past-before-the-past either remains outside the scope of the story or is summarized by the narrator, as in James's *What Maisie Knew*, which begins with a straight-forward journalistic introduction to the main characters and the plot,[9] or The Wings of the Dove, where the beginning is clearly Kate's encounter with Densher in the subway compartment:

> That had been the real beginning—the beginning of everything else; the other time, the time at the party, had been but the beginning of *that.*
> (*WD* 50)

But in *The Turn of the Screw* the beginning is supplanted by a lack of a beginning. Part of this past is recovered by the frame.

James judged his "*amusette*" much better framed than consistent and complete—better, that is, without a beginning. The Preface begins by denouncing "mere 'modern' psychical case[s]" like that with which the Prologue begins and which it promises the tale itself will transcend (*TS* 118). James's Preface thus makes it clear that anything added to the story itself would have destroyed not only the confessional tone but also the unity, the "perfect homogeneity" of the tale (*TS* 117):

> On the surface there wasn't much, but another grain, none the less, would have spoiled the precious pinch addressed to its end as neatly as some modicum extracted from an old silver snuff box and held between finger and thumb. (*TS* 118)

The tension of the story depends on its starting where the action starts. When James first heard the story from the Archbishop of Canterbury,[10] it was merely a "shadow of a shadow" (*TS* 118), and his intention was for its context to remain obscure through "the process of adumbration" with which he expanded his shadow into a novella (*TS* 122). The extra information, the "fact[s] to be in possession of," could not be communicated by the story itself and had to remain, in James's view, detached.

But the Prologue is also "ill-detachable," "difficult to detach" (*TP* 59), and the reasons for this are more complicated. James liked nothing better than a good fairy-tale: he writes in the Preface to "The Altar of the Dead" that "the 'ghost-story,' as we for convenience call it, has ever been for me the most probable form of the fairy-tale" (*AN* 254). In the Preface to *The Turn of the Screw* he writes that

> The charm of all these [fairy tales] for the distracted modern mind is in the clear field of experience, as I call it, over which we are thus led to roam; an annexed but independent world in which nothing is right save as we rightly imagine it. (*TS* 119)

The world of fairy tales, a "clear field of experience . . . annexed and independent," is the world that James had in mind when he created *The Turn of the Screw*, but to be "annexed" and "independent," this world requires a frame. The "clear field" of the governess's story of the children and the ghosts, "a fairy tale pure and simple" (*TS* 119), is framed, surrounded, and supported by a lively Christmas Eve of story telling, a drama of

> the circle, one winter afternoon, round the hall-fire of a grave old country-house where (for all the world as if to resolve itself promptly and obligingly into convertible, into "literary" stuff) the talk turned . . . to apparitions and night-fears, to the marked and sad drop in the general supply . . . of such commodities. (*TS* 117)

The romance of the fairy tale is emphasized and heightened by juxtaposition with the drama of the frame. The story is framed for the same reason that it is ambiguous: to exaggerate the romance of the story and prevent it from becoming a drama, "a mere modern psychical case."

On another level, the reason that the Prologue is necessary involves the differences between speech and writing. Goetz writes that the main difference between the Prologue and the story itself is that the former is oral and therefore privileged, the latter merely written. By claiming that the oral Prologue is privileged over the story itself, which is merely written, Goetz invokes the traditional hierarchy of the primacy of speech that deconstruction has rebelled against: he claims that the story proper depends upon the oral flexibility of the Prologue. But this solid inaccessibility of the tale is evidence more of the primacy of writing than of speech. The Prologue is a noisier and more dramatic piece of writing than the story it prefaces. When the Prologue begins, the manuscript, which the narrator has entitled *The Turn of the Screw*, is inaccessible, impenetrable, and silent, in "a locked drawer" (*TS* 2), and it must be made accessible by Douglas's servant in town. This impenetrability is a feature of all writing, and the juxtaposition of the tale with the Prologue emphasizes it by way of contrast. The Prologue, like the story, is also a written account, written down long after the events it describes take place. It describes an oral encounter with the impenetrability of writing, as does the story itself, in which letters that should be written simply are not and letters that are written are either not read or misinterpreted.[11] The permanence and incompleteness of writing are celebrated in James's story: the purpose of the frame is to uphold this incompleteness. The audience, who keep interrupting Douglas with annoying oversimplifications, are repressed and ancillary in the text; most of them are phased out of the text altogether:

> The departing ladies who said they would stay didn't, of course, stay: they departed in a rage of curiosity. (*TS* 4)

Douglas does his best to ignore the excitement of the women: "He took no notice of her," the narrator recalls after one of them interrupts, "he looked at me, but as if, instead of me, he saw what he spoke of" (*TS* 2). Douglas soon becomes absorbed by the story he reads, ignoring the women and their impertinent comments and even ignoring the narrator, whom he clearly has some reason to respect above the others in the group.[12] Even Douglas himself disappears: as the narrator summarizes Douglas's 'prologue,' Douglas is himself absorbed into oblivion by the manuscript he reads, and soon after the Prologue itself disappears, absorbed into the text and forgotten. It is a parergon:

> It disappears, buries itself, effaces itself, melts away at the moment it deploys its greatest energy. (*TP* 61)

It is appropriate that James's greatest ghost story is a text in which the written word, like death, is dominant and speech, the living drama of the frame, is dispensable. The purpose of the juxtaposition, though, is less to sustain a hierarchic relationship between writing and speech (or, from the reader's point of view, between reading and listening), than to unite them, to fuse them together.[13] The effect is a combined text with the permanence of a manuscript and the immediacy of a fire-side ghost story. This fusion of writing and speech, spiced with a vague touch of the past-perfect, is accomplished in the last line of the Prologue:

> But Douglas, without heeding me, had begun to read with a fine clearness that was like a rendering to the ear of the beauty of his author's hand. (*TS* 6)

The frame of James's *The Turn of the Screw* thus fits much better than critics have claimed. It is not perfect, of course: one of the mysteries of the novella, as Graham McMaster points out, is the question of whether the governess is ever punished for her failure to protect the children and how she supported herself thereafter—she would have needed, one would imagine, letters of recommendation to have gotten the job as governess to Douglas's sister. These details, unlike the nature of the ghosts, are facts that Douglas surely would have known, but he gives no answers. The Prologue as parergon, however, is complete and effective; if nothing else, it raises so many more questions than it answers that one is forced to re-read the Prologue after finishing the tale, and it thus serves as an epilogue as well. The Prologue thus heightens the ending of the tale and eliminates the need for a beginning; as an ill-detachable detachment it frames the immediacy of the story and accentuates it while providing necessary background information in a way that does not encroach upon the story. It is indispensable here for all the same reasons that Miriam Rooth must dispense with it in *The Tragic Muse.*

CHAPTER III

What Maisie Knew: Domestic Labyrinth and Human Frame

> Dictionaries most often give "hord-d'oeuvre," which is the strictest translation, but also "accessory, foreign or secondary object," "supplement," "aside," "remainder." It is what the principal object *must not become*, by being separated from itself: the education of children in legislation (*Laws* 766a) or the definition of science (*Thaeatetus* 184a) *must not* be treated as *parerga*.
>
> Jacques Derrida, *Parergon*[1]

In James's later works the frame plays a more vital and less abstract role than in his earlier ones. I have tried to clarify above the delicacy with which *The Turn of the Screw* is framed by its Prologue, but the dynamic value of the theory of the frame for the artist resides in the fact that it can operate as a relation between people as easily as between elements of a work of art. *What Maisie Knew* best exemplifies this aspect of the parergon.

Reading *The Turn of the Screw* and *What Maisie Knew* together, perhaps because they were written at much the same time,[2] yields surprising results with implications that illuminate the readings of each novel separately. My reading of *Maisie* begins with the extent to which the situation of *The Turn of the Screw* is reversed in it: Like Miles and Flora, Maisie Farange is a child whose absent parents are replaced by governesses, but her story is seen from the point of view of the child, rather than from that of the governess. In the early chapters Maisie's parents and governesses are as bizarre as the ghosts in *The Turn of the Screw. What Maisie Knew* thus begins as a ghost story, its eerie "turn of the screw" being that Maisie cannot even see the ghosts that haunt her existence. The point at which Maisie comes to realize the ghastliness of her guardians, which I will call the fairy-tale section of the novel, Chapters 17-21, is thus the turning point of the novel.

There is much laughter in the novel, most of it directed at Maisie. The young Maisie is a clown, "a figure mainly to be laughed at" (*WMK* 50), and the adults around her, particularly the gentlemen, never tire of picking on her:

> They pulled and pinched, they teased and tickled her; some of them even, as they termed it, shied things at her, and all of them thought it funny to call her by names having no resemblance to her own. (*WMK* 57)

Maisie is batted back and forth like a "shuttlecock" by her parents (*WMK* 42), and to their friends she is a plaything. Their laughter supplies Maisie with an identity—it is as if she were perpetually on stage, and no one laughs more often than Sir Claude, whose laughter, to Maisie, "was an indistinguishable part of the sweetness of his being there" (*WMK* 70).[3] It is ironic that in a book about knowledge and the death of childhood[4] the adults laugh hardest when Maisie knows something she shouldn't: "Even her profundity had left a margin for a laugh" (*WMK* 80). Her knowledge, which she has no idea she even possesses, is what makes her so funny to the adults around her.

The viciousness of the humor of the early chapters, however, derives from the fact that Maisie herself does not get any of the jokes.[5] These early chapters are laden with irony that seems heavy-handed and almost clumsy, on a first reading: we are told again and again that Maisie's parents' divorce unites them far more effectively than their marriage ever did and that each basks in the infamy of the affair. Maisie's parents' attitudes toward her are exactly reversed after the divorce: now each pushes Maisie toward the other instead of tugging her away as they had done during the litigation:[6]

> [Ida's] conscience winced under the acuteness of a candid friend who had remarked that the real end of all their tugging would be that each parent would try to make the little girl a burden to the other. (*WMK* 46)

The result of these role-reversals is that contradictions come to appear natural to Maisie; she is young and has no basis on which to object to them. She comes to accept contradictions and to be comfortable with irony and paradox, failing even to distinguish between truth and fiction: "She was at the age for which all stories are true and all conceptions are stories. The actual was the absolute, the present alone was vivid" (*WMK* 42). Since the irony of her situation is too overwhelming for her ever to perceive it as such, she accepts it, acquiring

> the positive certitude, bequeathed from afar by Moddle, that the natural way for a child to have her parents was separate and successive, like her mutton and her pudding or her bath and her nap. (*WMK* 44)

The pleasure the reader takes in her situation is a pleasure from which Maisie herself is excluded, and she accepts the string of almost preternatural governesses to whom she is subjected without doubt, suspicion, or regret.

A catalogue of the adults in Maisie's life is enough to show their similarity to the ghosts in *The Turn of the Screw.* After the divorce Maisie's world takes on a strangeness that she herself can hardly appreciate. "Her little world was phantasmagoric—strange shadows dancing on a sheet" (*WMK* 41),[7] but the shades and the forms are all the same to Maisie, who has no idea that she is buried in the depths of Plato's cave. The first ghostly governess to drift into her new life after Moddle, who had taken care of her before the divorce, is Miss Overmore, "on whose loveliness, as she supposed it, the little girl was faintly conscious that one couldn't rest with quite the same tucked-in and kissed-for-goodnight feeling" that she had been accustomed to with Moddle (*WMK* 50). Miss Overmore, "the pretty one" (*WMK* 52), rolls her eyes at Maisie and is simply beautiful. Maisie seems aware that, like Miles and Flora, there is something strange about her, but she accepts this strangeness without question: Miss Overmore is thus her introduction to both the social ambiguity of the station of governesses in late-Victorian England and the ambiguity of Maisie's own standing in the family. Maisie knows that Miss Overmore is "a lady, and yet awfully poor," as was often the case with Victorian governesses, and she also knows that "nursery-governesses were only for little girls who were not, as she said, 'really' little" (*WMK* 44). Miss Overmore is less bizarre than some of the other guardians Maisie is to have, but through her Maisie is introduced to the strange reality that lurks behind the appearances she is presented with: Maisie is unaware of the real reason that Miss Overmore follows her to Beale's household and of the strange relationship she is to have with Maisie's father under the guise of an employment that "he appreciates *immensely*" (*WMK* 47).[8] She does seem to know, however, and to accept, that there is a real reason that she is not to know about: "Everything had something behind it: life was like a long, long corridor with rows of closed doors. She had learned that at these doors it was not wise to knock" (*WMK* 54).

The eerie quality of Maisie's other governesses is clear to her: "She vaguely knew, further, somehow, that the future was still bigger than she, and that part of what made it so was the number of governesses lurking in it ready to dart out" (*WMK* 44). And dart out they do. Before Miss Overmore joins Beale Farange's household permanently Maisie is taken briefly into the hands of "a fat dark lady with a foreign name and dirty fingers," a "strange apparition" that "faded before the bright creature who had braved everything for Maisie's sake" (*WMK* 47). Miss Overmore "the bright creature" is next, and she is then replaced at Ida's by the motherly Mrs Wix, a "horrid beetle," who, with her diadem, her "dingy rosette like a large button," and her "straighteners" (*WMK* 49), is present to Maisie even in her absence throughout the novel:

> Her very silence became after this one of the largest elements of Maisie's consciousness; it proved a warm and habitable air, into which the child penetrated farther than she ever dared to mention to her companions. Somewhere in the depths of it the dim straighteners were fixed upon her; somewhere out of the troubled little current Mrs Wix intently waited.
> (*WMK* 60)[9]

Mrs Wix is upstaged by the most phantasmagoric ghost of all, "little dead Clara Matilda, who, on a crossing in the Harrow Road, was knocked down and crushed to death by the cruelest of hansoms" (*WMK* 49). Clara, Maisie's "little dead sister" who "wasn't a real sister, but that only made her more romantic," takes on a ghostly reality to Maisie, who "knew everything about her that could be known, everything she had said or done in her little mutilated life" (*WMK* 49). Clara is as present to Maisie's fecund imagination as any of her governesses are, and Maisie seems to accept her as a member of the family, just as she accepts her obviously flawed governesses without question. Even Lisette, her doll, comes alive, and Maisie builds a world of mystery and ambiguity for her that reflects her own.

These ghosts are real to Maisie in their incoherence, like the "intensive particulars" that, according to Jean Frantz Blackall, comprise Maisie's earliest consciousness of the world (Blackall 133). The point is not so much that they are ghostly as that they are ghastly, like monsters in a romance, and would doubtless appear so to Maisie if she had not grown up surrounded by them. But she accepts reality and fiction together as equals and does not distinguish between them or prefer one to the other. Her world, like Bly, is teeming with ghosts, but Maisie, unlike the governess in *The Turn of the Screw*, is too innocent to object to them.

When Maisie's parents remarry a frame-like structure emerges out of this world of phantoms, a neat quincuncial system of tugs and shoves, and in a sense Maisie's four parents and stepparents, who are always trying to "square" each other, form a frame around our portrait of Maisie. What Maisie lacks and desperately needs, of course, is parents, and if Maisie's guardians would perform the roles that they pretend to perform, they would constitute a frame. But all these possible parents are replaced by ghastly governesses: "Parents had come to seem vague, but governesses were evidently to be trusted" (*WMK* 59). We would like to see Maisie nurtured and supported by some combination of her guardians, buttressed by them as a painting is braced and sustained by its frame, but the quincuncial structure calls attention to the fact that she clearly derives none of the benefits of a frame from them—as Derrida notes, "not every milieu, even if it is contiguous with the work, constitutes a *parergon*" (*TP* 59). If Maisie is ever framed by her parents' remarriages, the affair between Mrs Beale and Sir Claude begins to erode the frame as soon as it is constructed. Maisie's world subdivides too quickly for her to choose sides; she is simply in the middle, surrounded by the chaos of adultery:

> If it had become now, for that matter, a matter of sides, there was at least a certain amount of evidence as to where they all were. Maisie, of course, in such a delicate position, was on nobody's; . . . (*WMK* 93)

Maisie's frame, if so it may be called, is a fluid one; as soon as her parents remarry their marriages begin to deteriorate.[10]

Maisie's own role, I suggest, is that of a parergon: she is not an integral part of the family, but she frames it. Though Maisie does not understand her father's relationship with Miss Overmore, she does see that she is herself the "awfully proper reason" that they are able to contrive the arrangement (*WMK* 53). Miss Overmore's presence in the Farange household depends upon Maisie:

> She was in a false position and so freely and loudly called attention to it that it seemed to become almost a source of glory. (*WMK* 56)

Though Maisie is unwanted, she is necessary; the family would collapse without her. Maisie is given the credit for bringing her stepparents together, just as she "did it" to Mrs Beale and her father (*WMK* 74), but she is actually no more or less than "a jolly good pretext" (*WMK* 154) that the adults cling to in order to prevent the world from seeing what they are really doing.[11] Like the frame of a painting, Maisie appears from a distance to be a part of the family, but from within it she is a complication for which there is no place; she is an excluded but necessary pretext. Maisie, like the column that holds up a building, is both necessary and excluded from the goings-on inside. She is a parergon, "the great alternative to the proper" (*WMK* 58). Without Maisie, her father and Miss Overmore would be exposed as adulterers. The lack that necessitates the frame, then, is simply the lack of decency. A presence is required to atone for this absence, and Maisie is that presence.

In *What Maisie Knew* James portrays a world in which adults use each other without scruple. Maisie's innocence is parergonal in *What Maisie Knew* because it is so useful, and we can thus draw a parallel between adulthood, which collapses under the weight of its own lack of constraints, and the painting that requires a frame in order to be presentable. Adulthood is thus incomplete: it cannot sustain itself or realize its moral ideal without the pretext of a frame. Dennis Foster has this incompleteness in mind when he writes of Mrs Beale that "when she speaks, her language betrays the attempt of the unconscious to erase the conflict between socially acceptable and socially unacceptable roles, between wife and mistress" (Foster 212). Camille Paglia's comparison of the irony in *The Wings of the Dove* to "a hedgehog rooting about under a doily" (Paglia 608) comes to mind also—in this case Maisie is the doily. The inside of the work, actual family life, is not compatible with the outside, strict Victorian morality, and thus they must be separated and reconciled by a frame. Maisie is that frame, and she is a brilliant one; she is successful in making her parents worthy of our attention. As James remarked in the Preface,

> The great thing is indeed that the muddled state too is one of the very sharpest of the realities, that it also has color and form and character, has often in fact a broad and rich comicality, many of the signs and values of the appreciable.[12] (*WMK* 30)

All this time, of course, Maisie's education is being neglected, but this unfortunate consequence of her parergonality is rationalized away by her guardians: Mrs Beale exclaims to her, "'It isn't as if you didn't already know everything, is it, love?'" (*WMK* 80). Maisie's apparent innocence is what makes her so valuable, but it is assumed from the start that Maisie has no real innocence and never has had any. What she derives from her experience of life, then, is "an innocence saturated with knowledge" (*WMK* 150). Since she does not yet completely understand the motivations of her elders, her education consists not of knowledge at all but of a fine sharpening of her ability to deal with ambiguity: she learns, as it were, to reason with ghosts. Maisie is the margin between the inside and the outside of her family, and as such she is distant from both, a lonely child kept upstairs surrounded, as Paul Armstrong has observed, by "a prison of ambiguity" (Armstrong 520), by the irony of jokes she does not understand.[13] She is at home in the midst of ambiguity and nothing makes her shine so brightly, but a prison is not a frame. Maisie is separated from the irony of her situation in the first half of the novel as if by a pane of glass, and she has the feeling that she is watching her own story unfold as through a window:

> So the sharpened sense of spectatorship was the child's main support, the long habit, from the first, of seeing herself in discussion and finding in the fury of it—she had had a glimpse of the game of football—a sort of compensation

> for the doom of a peculiar passivity. It gave her often an odd air of being present at her history in as separate a manner as if she could only get at experience by flattening her nose against a pane of glass. (*WMK* 101)

The image of Maisie with her nose against the glass is repeated later, where she still feels "as if she were flattening her nose upon the hard window-pane of the sweet-shop of knowledge" (*WMK* 120). Maisie is separated from her own history by an invisible barrier in the same way that a frame is separated from a painting by a crack. The real action of the novel—the sordid intrigue and romance between Maisie's various guardians and their various lovers—is vague and implied; it recedes into the background. Our attention is focused on Maisie, who understands fully none of her parents motivations but at the same time is a pretext for them. Insofar as it is a portrait of a young lady *What Maisie Knew* is thus a painting of a frame.[14]

I want to focus on the portion of the novel that comes just before the end, Chapters 17-21, which I call the fairy-tale section. This section is the turning point of the novel: it is here that Maisie ceases to be necessary to her parents, whereupon they both return to her to enact a ceremony of detachment from their daughter, a ceremony in which Maisie is an active participant. Maisie is left behind like a frame without a picture. Her perception of the world begins to change during the tumultuous fairy-tale section of the book, a section that Maisie herself recognizes as "a new phase" (*WMK* 137), beginning with what James called in the Preface "the inevitable shift . . . of her point of view" (*WMK* 28). It begins with the trip to the Great Exhibition in Earl's Court, "an extemporized expensive treat" (*WMK* 146), and ends with the migration to France. It is like a dream vision for Maisie, in which the phantasmagoric world of her early childhood returns to torment her. The glass barrier of her innocence gradually disappears and Maisie's parents, hitherto distant, return to her like the bizarre characters in the stories of her childhood, suddenly near enough to touch. Her parents and her childhood return to her together, as it were, as if to say goodbye.[15]

Strange tales and stories have formed a large part of Maisie's education: Maisie, we are reminded in Chapter 17,

> had been in thousands of stories—all Mrs Wix's and her own, to say nothing of the richest romances of the French Elise—but she had never been in such a story as this. . . . The Arabian Nights had quite closed round her.
>
> From this minute that pitch of the wondrous was in everything. (*WMK* 145)

Sir Claude is "her good fairy" (*WMK* 136), and the money the Countess tosses to Maisie is "too much even for a fee in a fairy tale" (*WMK* 159). After the Exhibition, in the Countess's house, Maisie finds a surreal world of colors and flowers, silence and light, and feathers and chocolates. She is awed by the turbulent changes her world is going through, and in the chaos she sees for the first time those around her, particularly her parents, as the monsters they are. Thomas Jeffers (quoting Martha Banta) has written of the fairy-tale chapters that "the Shakespearean 'green world' metamorphoses into a Jacobean funny-terrible freak show, a debased amusement park inhabited not by simple nymphs but by bejeweled nymphomaniacs" (Jeffers 160). The colorful narration corresponds directly to Maisie's increased sensitivity to the world around her—unknown to the adults, Maisie is becoming more aware of her situation at the same time that it is encroaching more closely than ever upon her. If these chapters are dreamlike for Maisie, they are a carnival of delights for the reader and constitute the most humorous and vivid part of the novel. Maisie has begun the process of metamorphosis from a frame to a work. And it is in the fairy-tale section that Maisie first has the chance to apply her knowledge.

The fairy-tale section, in which Maisie's parents, no longer united so neatly by their hatred of each other, return to her separately and force her to renounce them and absolve them of their guilt, is appropriately divided by a period of five days into two parts, one for each parent. In the first part, in the Exhibition, Beale emerges from "the Flowers of the Forest" with the Countess, a woman who "might have been a clever frizzled poodle in a frill or a dreadful human monkey in a spangled petticoat" (*WMK* 156). We have seen little more of Beale Farange (whose surname was to be "Hurter" when James originally conceived of the story)[16] than his haunting beard and teeth in the first half of the novel, but he suddenly reappears in Chapter 18 as a befanged beast:

> There was a passage during which [her father's "foolish awkwardness"], on a yellow silk sofa under one of the palms, he had her on his knee stroking her hair, playfully holding her off while he showed her his shining fangs and let her, with a vague affectionate helpless pointless 'Dear old girl, dear little daughter,' inhale the fragrance of his cherished beard. She must have been sorry for him, she afterwards knew, so well could she privately follow his difficulty in being specific to her about anything. (*WMK* 148)

Beale is harmless, however, defeated by the awkwardness of his guilt, and Maisie knows it. Maisie clearly knows exactly what her father is trying to do with her, but she is devoid in this passage of all the emotions she might be expected to feel in the presence of her sordid father. She feels pity, but no fear or shame:

> There was something in him that seemed, and quite touchingly, to ask her to help him to pretend—pretend he knew enough about her life and her education, her means of subsistence and her view of himself, to give the questions he couldn't put her a natural domestic tone. She would have pretended with ecstasy if he could only have given her the cue. (*WMK* 149)

Beale has never been enough a part of Maisie's life for her to regret his desertion of her; to her he is merely an associate who feels it is time to disconnect. She tries, though unsuccessfully, to pretend along with her father, and she feels sympathy for his awkward predicament. Maisie tries as much as possible to help ease the process of his making her repudiate him but she feels no remorse or regret: she only understands. Her father is using her, and he is frustrated by the fact that he might have been able to continue using her if things had worked out differently:

> When he had lighted a cigarette and begun to smoke in her face it was as if he had struck with the match the note of some queer clumsy ferment of old professions, old scandals, old duties, a dim perception of what he possessed in her and what, if everything had only—damn it!—been totally different, she might still be able to give him. (*WMK* 148-9)

The "it was as if" and the "damn it!" here indicate the extent to which Maisie is extrapolating from her father's words and make it clear that she understands what her father wants her to do. Like Lionel Croy in *The Wings of the Dove* who wants "to give [Kate] up with some style and state" (*WD* 25), Beale wants Maisie to repudiate him and he wants to appear magnanimous while she does it. Again Maisie extrapolates:

> It was exactly as if he had broken out to her: 'I say, you little booby, help me to be irreproachable, to be noble, and yet to have none of the beastly bore of it. There's only impropriety enough for one of us; so *you* must take it all. *Repudiate* your dear old daddy—in the face, mind you, of his tender supplications. He can't be rough with you—it isn't in his nature: therefore you'll have successfully chucked him because he was too generous to be as firm with you, poor man, as was, after all, his duty. (*WMK* 153)

Maisie responds at her sharpest: she even lies to him, promising "'I'll do anything in the world you ask me, papa'" (*WMK* 152). Her impression of him is compared to "one of the pantomimes to which Sir Claude had taken her: she saw nothing in it but what it conveyed" (*WMK* 156), but the astounding thing is that Maisie plays along with her father's pantomime. Regardless of her understanding of the nature of adultery, Maisie pities her father, proving that whatever it is that she knows, she understands him better than he has ever understood her.

Five days later, after a near-revolution in her father's household, Maisie is whisked off after breakfast to Folkstone, which "swim[s] in a softness of color and sound" (*WMK* 164) and which is for Maisie a "paradise" (*WMK* 170):

> Maisie had known all along a great deal, but never so much as she was to know from this moment on and as she learned in particular during the couple of days that she was to hang in the air, as it were, over the sea which represented in breezy blueness and with a summer charm a crossing of more spaces than the channel. (*WMK* 162)

In Folkstone she finds ecstasy and wonder, miracle and sacrifice, and her contumelious mother reappears in all her glory. Maisie and her step-father are sitting together in the garden of the hotel, surveying "the human scene" when the "apparition" appears (*WMK* 166):

> Sir Claude, beside her, was occupied with a cigarette and the afternoon papers; and though the hotel was full the garden showed the particular void that ensues upon the sound of the dressing bell. She had almost had time to weary of the human scene; her own humanity at any rate, in the shape of a smutch on her scanty skirt, had held her so long that as soon as she raised her eyes they rested on a high fair drapery by which smutches were put to shame and which had glided towards her over the grass without her noting its rustle. She followed up its stiff sheen—up and up from the ground, where it had stopped—till at the end of a considerable journey her impression felt the shock of a fixed face which, surmounting it, seemed to offer the climax of the dressed condition. 'Why mamma!' she cried the next instant. (*WMK* 166)

If her father reappeared as a dragon her mother arrives on the scene as a towering gliding ghost—it is as if each, still, strives to attain the sublimity that will render the other ridiculous. Again, however, Maisie somehow knows exactly what her parent has come to do, and she seems almost embarrassed to have caught her proud mother in the undignified position of arranging her own renunciation:

> She had the positive sense of... catching their relative, catching her in the act of getting rid of her burden with a finality that showed her as unprecedentedly relaxed. (*WMK* 167)

Ida, too, wants to be repudiated, but Maisie feels no resentment toward her mother for preparing to desert her; rather, she sees Ida as an attractive and desirable person worthy of sympathy and respect:

> [Ida's] huge eyes, her red lips, the intense marks in her face formed an *éclairage* as distinct and public as a lamp set in a window. The child seemed

> quite to see in it the very beacon that had lighted her path; she suddenly found herself reflecting that it was no wonder the gentlemen were guided. (*WMK* 168-69)

Maisie feels no fear or intimidation at her mother's presence. She even stands up to Ida on the issue of her precious Captain, but she is not without feeling for her mother and looks on Ida with the kindness and understanding of a grateful daughter, knowing that she

> had not come to box any ears or to bang any doors or even to use any language: she had come at the worst to lose the thread of her argument in an occasional dumb twitch of the toggery in which Mrs Beale's low domestic had had the impudence to serve up Miss Farange. (*WMK* 173)

Again, the phrase "as if" is used to show how vividly Maisie understands her mother's tone; Maisie translates and explains to herself what her mother is really trying to say, just as she had done with her father:

> It was as if she had said in so many words: 'There have been things between us,—between Sir Claude and me—which I needn't go into, you little nuisance, because you wouldn't understand them. (*WMK* 173)

This is not to say, of course, that Maisie knows what these "things" between them are. Again, as in the interview with her father, Maisie seems to lack a complete understanding of her mother's motivations: "her impatience itself made at instants the whole situation swim; there were things Ida said that she perhaps didn't hear, and there were things she heard that perhaps Ida didn't say" (*WMK* 174). Maisie is interpreting and participating in her mother's pantomime of desertion. She is aware that her own role has long been that of a parergonal pretext, and she is no longer interested in playing that role. But she wants to play it quickly and meekly to the end by assisting her parents in severing all connections with her: as a frame she is still careful not to upstage her parents' performances. She wants to "complete the good work and set her ladyship so promptly and majestically afloat as to leave the great seaway clear for the morrow" (*WMK* 175). Maisie has big plans for the Continent, and she is relieved that her parents will no longer be around to complicate things for her.

Maisie sees the part she has been playing in the drama of her guardians' games, and though she may not be able to see beyond the pantomime to the rotten core, her understanding of the situation is profoundly accurate:

> The relation between her step-parents had then a mysterious residuum: this was the first time she had reflected that except as regards herself it was not a relationship. (*WMK* 141).

Maisie becomes aware, in the fairy-tale section, that Mrs Beale and Sir Claude are lovers (*WMK* 163-64), and this discovery helps her to understand the residuary nature of her own existence: she is simply matter remaining at the end of the process of her parents' and step-parents' manipulations of each other. The works, the adulterous couples, are removed from the frame, and Maisie is left behind like a noxious by-product, outgrown and discarded. Maisie realizes that she has long been knowingly "compromised" by her parents, and though she tries to fool her parents by continuing to play the role of the unwitting victim, she is "much more of a little person to reckon with" (*WMK* 148) because she has learned how to deceive. In the fairy-tale chapters Maisie, the ill-detachable detachment, participates in her own "detachment" from her parents (*WMK* 151, 159). It is in these chapters Maisie ceases to be a frame.

The tone of the later chapters of *What Maisie Knew* is radically different from that in the beginning of the novel. The supreme irony of the fairy-tale section is that it is so eerie precisely because it is so real. The people have not changed but Maisie has come to see them as they are, and this new vision accounts for the great change in the tone of the novel. "The polished plate of filial superstition" (*WMK* 173), like the window pane of Maisie's innocence, is fractured by her understanding of her situation, and this process of revelation is horrifying: "there was literally an instant in which Maisie saw—saw madness and desolation, saw ruin and darkness and death" (*WMK* 177). At the end of Chapter 20 Sir Claude is free, and Maisie shares his freedom ecstatically. She is free, in her own eyes at least, of her wretched childhood:

> After dinner she smoked with her friend—for that was exactly what she thought she did—on a porch, a kind of terrace, where the red tips of cigars and the light dresses of ladies made, under the happy stars, a poetry that was almost intoxicating. (*WMK* 180)

Maisie is free, and she is determined to hold on to her freedom. The scope of the novel has expanded as a result of Maisie's new determination: townspeople, virtually absent from the early chapters, are now described with clarity. The French *patronne*, for instance, is painted brilliantly with the extended metaphor of a clock on the mantle:

> a lady turned to [Sir Claude] from the bustling, breezy hall a countenance covered with fresh matutinal powder and a bosom as capacious as the velvet

shelf of a chimney-piece, over which her round white face, framed in its golden frizzle, might have figured as a showy clock. (*WMK* 239)

a very old personage with a red ribbon in his button-hole, whose manner of soaking buttered rolls in coffee and then disposing of them in the little that was left of the interval between his nose and chin might at a less anxious hour have cast upon Maisie an almost envious spell. (*WMK* 240)

We find towards the end of the book, also, the brilliantly melodramatic dialogue that we expect from James and of which the earlier chapters are devoid.[17] In Boulogne, Maisie is overcome with emotion, with "the great ecstasy of a larger impression of life" (*WMK* 181):

She was 'abroad' and she gave herself up to it, responded to it, in the bright air, before the pink houses, among the bare-legged fish-wives and the red-legged soldiers, with the instant certitude of a vocation. Her vocation was to see the world and to thrill with the enjoyment of the picture. (*WMK* 181)

No longer called upon to frame her guardians, Maisie becomes an observer of the world and thus, perhaps unwittingly, enters the realm of adulthood. Maisie finds her "initiation" (*WMK* 181) in the French breakfast, and she immediately changes roles in her relationship with Susan Ash, becoming an explainer like her mother and showing Susan around town. One gets the feeling that she has just entered the world for the first time from its margins: "she recognized, she understood, she adored and took possession; feeling herself attuned to everything and laying her hand, right and left, on what had simply been waiting for her" (*WMK* 182). Ostensibly, of course, and ironically, Maisie is no longer seeing as clearly as she did in the fairy-tale chapters. She now is living a fantasy, a dream in which Sir Claude is her shining knight and Paris is "the *real* thing" (*WMK* 182). Maisie's "heart was not at all in the gossip about Boulogne; and if her complexion was partly the result of the déjeuner and the *petits verres* it was also the brave signal of what she was there to say" (*WMK* 186). Maisie is in France to see and to say, neither of which she ever had the chance to do as a parergonal pretext in a prison of ambiguity: she is "coming out" (*WMK* 230).

Maisie, long stuck like the frame of a picture as if on a different plane of existence, is conscious in Boulogne of having shed her old role as pretext and is determined to make the most of her new opportunity. Her freedom, however, is short-lived. She clearly cannot sustain her freedom alone, and by the time of Mrs Wix's return in Chapter 22 the groundwork is already laid for the choice Maisie will soon have to make between the adults that remain. Ida has sent Mrs Wix to Boulogne to keep Maisie and Sir Claude decent: "'It's to *keep* you decent that I'm here and that I've done everything that I have done'" (*WMK* 192). Mrs Wix, in other words, is now to play Maisie's usual role by framing Maisie and her stepfather from the public scrutiny—this is ironic both because governess and (step)daughter have changed roles and because framing is probably not necessary in France in the first place. Mrs Wix is back, "proving more of a force to reckon with than either of them had allowed so much room for" (*WMK* 200). She delivers her moral teachings with "an unparalleled neigh of battle" (*WMK* 196) and with "a great giggling insinuating naughty slap" to Sir Claude's face (*WMK* 197): "'nobody, you know, is free to commit a crime'" (*WMK* 207), she reminds them. Mrs Wix is a fearless avenger with "a certain greatness" (*WMK* 210), fighting for Maisie's now famous "moral sense" (*WMK* 211).

Sir Claude and Mrs Beale, on the other hand, have decidedly not changed, though they appear different to Maisie. Sir Claude pays Maisie and Mrs Wix to let him return to Mrs Beale (*WMK* 199), and he pays Ida to cease to be Maisie's mother (*WMK* 228). Mrs. Beale, later, uses Maisie to make Sir Claude return to Boulogne (*WMK* 220). Mrs. Beale tries to entice Maisie with plans of a trip to the Etablissement, but Maisie is wary enough to expect little more than a repeat performance of the abortive trip to the Great Exhibition: "the francs failed like the shillings and the side-shows had set an example to the concert. The Etablissement in short melted away" (*WMK* 227). The end of the novel is made up of a series of scenes in which Mrs Beale and Sir Claude parallel the behavior of Beale and Ida in the fairy-tale section with uncanny accuracy. Mrs Beale forces Maisie back into a role of secondary significance by glibly explaining the mechanics of the settlement between Sir Claude and Ida in which "'she lets him off supporting her if he'll let her off supporting you'" (*WMK* 228). Mrs Beale even becomes Maisie's guide to the Continent, telling stories of her childhood travels that Maisie has heard so often in her own childhood that they have "with time become phantasmal" (*WMK* 227): her parents are trying to become her parents and to use her as Beale and Ida had done. Sir Claude, after a smooth string of lies,[18] confides in Maisie separately, just as Beale had done in the Countess's apartments. Mrs Wix insists that without Maisie Sir Claude will be destroyed: "'He'll have got nothing, He'll have lost everything. It will be his utter destruction, for he's certain after a while to loathe her [Mrs Beale]'" (*WMK* 233-34), and this warning proves valid when Sir Claude gives his speech at the café over breakfast the next morning:

> "I've been awfully worried, and this's what it has come to. You've done us the most tremendous good, and you'll do it still and always, don't you see? We

can't let you go—you're everything. There are the facts as I say. She *is* your mother now, Mrs Beale, by what has happened, and I, in the same way, I'm your father. No one can contradict that, and we can't get out of it . . ."
(*WMK* 247)

So Maisie finds herself again faced with the prospect of framing the indecency of her guardians. Sir Claude is worried about losing his freedom, and Maisie is thus everything to him. Like Chad and Madame de Vionnet in *The Ambassadors*, for whom "not being able to marry is all they've with any confidence to look forward to" (*TA* 169), Sir Claude is trying to avoid marriage and to appear "good" while doing so:

"My idea would be a nice little place—somewhere in the South—where she and you would be together and as good as anyone else. And I should be as good too, don't you see? for I shouldn't live with you, but I should be close to you—just round the corner, and it would be just the same. My idea would be that it should all be perfectly open and frank. *Honi soit qui mal y pense*, don't you know?" (*WMK* 247)

Sir Claude and Mrs Beale do not see marriage as a viable solution to the problem of their attraction toward one another. Marriage does not present itself to Maisie's stepparents, as it may to the reader, as the easy and obvious way of framing their adultery, though it is the only socially acceptable arrangement. Sir Claude's idea is simply to have for himself the benefits of a wife without the responsibilities and torments of a legal union. Adulthood, which as we have seen is a synonym for adultery in this novel, collapses without a frame in Victorian England, and Maisie is to be the frame of it once again: Maisie's new "parents," like Beale and Ida in the fairy-tale chapters, are forcing her, under the guise of freedom of choice, to support their immorality.

Maisie is aware of the situation she is confronted with in Boulogne and she knows she will have to make a choice, but she puts off her choice until the last minute. One of her alternatives is to agree to continue to frame adultery by accepting Sir Claude's proposition, remaining "equally associated and disconnected" (*WMK* 258) from her stepparents in parergonal suspension above and beyond the real world. Another choice Maisie considers, and which Sir Claude seems briefly to consider seriously as well, would make her an adulteress, at least in the eyes of the world. Her fantasy is to run off to Paris with Sir Claude, framed only by the newspapers and the pink and yellow novels that would serve for luggage:

She knew how prepared they looked to pass into the train, and she presently brought out to her companion: "I wish we could go. Won't you take me?"

He continued to smile. "Would you really come?"

> "Oh yes, oh yes. Try."
> "Do you want me to take our tickets?"
> "Yes, take them."
> "Without any luggage?"
> She showed their two armfuls, smiling at him as he smiled at her, but so conscious of being more frightened than she had ever been in her life that she seemed to see her whiteness as in a glass. Then she knew that what she saw was Sir Claude's whiteness: he was as frightened as herself. (*WMK* 253-54)

But her fantasy remains unfulfilled, and though her fear fades into the distance with the passing train, she clings to her fantasy till the end.

Fortunately for Maisie there is a third alternative; she is not simply forced to choose between framing two adulterers and becoming one herself. Mrs Wix, who has sacrificed her own innocence to protect Maisie's own, protests:

> "Don't let me pay for nothing; don't let me have been thrust for nothing into such horrors and such shames. I never knew anything about them and I never wanted to know! Now I know too much, too much!" (*WMK* 214)

Mrs Wix is thus the only person in the novel besides Maisie herself who has perceived the horrors of the fairy-tale chapters, and this shared perception is what links the two of them together in the end. Mrs Wix, also, still feels the pain of the daughter she lost to "the cruellest of hansoms," and Maisie likewise has not recovered from the recent loss of her mother. In the end she renounces both her fantasy and her role as a framing device and chooses simply to be a child. Maisie's choice of a mother over a business proposition is a sign, ironically, that she is growing up. James wrote of John Singer Sargent in 1887 that in spite of his great triumphs "his future is the most valuable thing he has to show" (Sargent 691). The same might, at the end of the book, be said of young Maisie Farange.

The beauty of Maisie Farange is that she never gives up. She never loses faith in her perception of the world, no matter how askew her interpretation may be, retaining "a small smug conviction that in the domestic labyrinth she always kept the clue" (*WMK* 90). Maisie does not, of course, hold the key to the labyrinth that imprisons her childhood, but her intuitive navigation of its passages is extraordinary. Maisie's intuition brings us back to the question critics of *What Maisie Knew* must try to answer, which is of course suggested by the title of the novel: what does Maisie know? She herself sees no limits to the amount of knowledge available to her, and her handling of her parents' desertion and her choice of a fresh new attempt at childhood in the end support her conviction:

> the very climax of the concatenation would . . . be the stage at which the knowledge should overflow. As she was condemned to know more and more, how could it logically stop before she should know Most? It came to her in fact as they sat there on the sands that she was distinctly on the road to know Everything. (*WMK* 213)

Inevitably the question of Maisie's knowledge depends upon the question of her morality. Foster has shown that if Maisie's guardians are immoral and Mrs Wix is moral, Maisie herself is amoral: "Maisie's moral sense never really includes an idea of good and evil" (Foster 210).[19] The immorality of Maisie's situation thus becomes an ethical curse but an epistemological blessing: it allows her to grow up without the often illogical constraints of popular morality to distract her from her ideal. Jeffers notes that "she posits this ideal as one might posit the idea of a God: it is the 'possible' she needs if she is to climb out of the fetid air of betrayal and recrimination she has breathed from the start" (Jeffers 167). There is no limit to Maisie's potential for knowledge because there is no limit placed upon her by morality. The same immorality that stifles her education launches her toward freedom. Maisie's amorality is what allows her to endure, and it is her endurance, as Foster and others have noted, that we like about her.

CHAPTER IV

The Ambassadors: The Oblong Gilt Frame

> But this tension, this vection, this rection is absolutely interrupted, with a clean blow. *It has to be* thus interrupted: by having to be, purely, absolutely, removing all adherence to what it cuts itself off from, it liberates beauty (free, wandering, and vague). By having to be interrupted, the *sans*-text and the *sans*-theme relate to the end in the mode of nonrelation. Absolute nonrelation. And by having to be so, this absolute nonrelation must also, if possible, be inscribed in the structure of the artifact.
>
> Jacques Derrida, *Parergon*[1]

The Ambassadors may represent James's most sophisticated use of the framing device in fiction. The frame of the novel, as I will show, is hidden both where one would least expect to find it and where it can play its role most profoundly: it is Chapters 30 and 31, the Lambinet chapters, and it contains the climax of the novel. An examination of the climax, in which Strether's imagination leads to his discovery of the truth behind the "virtuous attachment" between Chad and Madame de Vionnet, shows that what William Goetz calls the "fictional bounds of the text" (Goetz 187) are released: Strether escapes both into art and out of it, and that Strether is not wrecked by his imagination but rather saved by it.

But human frames are also at work in *The Ambassadors*. Maisie Farange's character and her function as frame are echoed in Jeanne de Vionnet, who to Strether is like a beautiful work of art:

> What was in the girl was indeed too soft, too unknown for direct dealing; so that one could only gaze at it as at a picture, quite staying one's own hand.
>
> She was fairly beautiful to him—a faint pastel in an oval frame: he thought of her already as of some lurking image in a long gallery, the portrait of a small old-time princess of whom nothing was known but that she had died young. (*TA* 134-35, 154)

Jeanne must, of course, somehow remind Strether of his son, who died a small boy, and he tries to remain as distant from his Parisian friends as he is from his son as if they are pictures instead of people. But though

Strether views Jeanne as a picture her function in the drama is that of a frame, as Maisie's is in her own "drama of figures" (*WMK* 180). Jeanne de Vionnet frames her mother's relations, at least to Strether, in much the same way that Maisie frames her father's, by acting as a decoy bride-to-be. She even echoes Maisie Farange's tone with her "'Mamma wishes me to tell you before we go . . . that she hopes very much that you'll come to see us very soon'" (*TA* 134). Jeanne de Vionnet is a frame, but Strether's fascination with her and his insistence on viewing her as a painting contrast ironically with James's own preoccupation with the parergonal and his interest in the relation between the work and the frame that is the focus of this essay.

James clearly preferred the quiet dignity of the frame to the audacity of the work, and the early chapters of *The Ambassadors* abound with evidence of this preference. Julie Rivkin has shown that "the supplement itself is a 'prime idea' in *The Ambassadors*" (Rivkin 384, note 6) as has Mary Ann Caws, who writes that "By the time of *The Ambassadors*, the aesthetic sense of border is openly of greater interest for James than the rather dreary 'plot'" (Caws 148). Lambert Strether, like Maisie, is a Jamesian hero who has been manipulated into the position of framing something more vulgar than himself: in the words of his friend Waymarsh he is "'a fine-tooth comb [used] to groom a horse'" (*TA* 74). "'You're being used for a thing you ain't fit for'" (*TA* 74), Waymarsh warns him. Mrs. Newsome, as if a literalization of Derrida's wheelchair metaphor, cannot support herself enough to realize her own desires and depends on Strether in much the same way that a work depends on a frame: "'Everything's too much for her'" (*TA* 47) Strether explains. Strether is being used as a proxy by Mrs. Newsome, and it is thus from her entirely that he derives the strength, sustenance, and sense of purpose of his "life of utility" (*TA* 153). In return, of course, Strether is Mrs. Newsome's contact with Paris and with her son, and it is only through Strether that she is able to view the action in Paris.[2] Strether redresses the lack of health in Mrs. Newsome—without her poor health and strength his own presence would be unnecessary; Maria Gostrey observes: "'I see it, her condition, as beneath and behind you; yet at the same time I see it as bearing you up'" (*TA* 47). Even before his trip to Europe, Strether was a frame to Mrs. Newsome's "Review" (*TA* 50), "'her tribute to the ideal'" (*TA* 51). His name, not hers, appears on the journal's green cover, and this frame has become Strether's "'one presentable little scrap of an identity'" (*TA* 51), so that he has become not an independent man of action but a static and obedient front for Mrs. Newsome's endeavors:

> He was Lambert Strether because he was on the cover, whereas it should have been, for anything like glory, that he was on the cover because he was Lambert Strether. (*TA* 62)

Though Strether is an effective supplement, however, he is an incomplete one because the only form of union between two people that is recognized in Woollett is the legal form. In America there is no such luxury as the "'virtuous attachment'" (*TA* 112) that Chad enjoys in Paris, and so Strether can attach himself to his remarkable associate only through marriage. Strether endures his subordinate frame-like position partly because of what Sarah Pocock calls his "essential inaptitude" (*TA* 105)[3] but mostly because he hopes to be remunerated for his efforts with marriage to the matriarch herself. He hopes, in essence, to attach himself to Mrs. Newsome and become a permanent frame, and his success in this endeavor will depend on his success in Paris. But *The Ambassadors* is much more fluid a novel than the quincuncial *What Maisie Knew*, and Strether, like Jeanne, soon loses interest in framing another person's inadequacies. When he arrives in Paris, Strether's goal of permanent, secure subordinateness is transformed by the taste of freedom, that elusive ideal, into a need for that quality that James describes in the Preface to *What Maisie Knew* as "appreciable."[4] The novel follows the thread of Strether's journey to primacy, his quest to become, in Madame de Vionnet's words, "'an object of interest'" (*TA* 320).

There are various stages in this process. Strether, "the hero of the drama" (*TA* 265), comes to see the world early on as a play in which his friends perform for him while he sits idly by and appreciates, and it is necessary at the outset to set the scene of that drama and to describe the situation Strether glides naively into on his arrival in Paris. As in *The Tragic Muse*, Drama is the metaphor through which much of the meaning of *The Ambassadors* is expressed:[5] Strether is an observer, or so he believes, seeing only what walks onto the stage of Parisian society in front of him, and he is left to guess about what it all means. In London Strether goes with Maria Gostrey to plays in the evening, and the stage, a world of types, becomes a metaphor of his experience of Europe:

> It was an evening, it was a world of types, and this was a connexion above all in which the figures and faces in the stalls were interchangeable with those on the stage. (*TA* 43)

The only "types" Woollett had recognized were "the male and the female" (*TA* 44), and people there are thus distinguished from one another only by their spouses. But "however he viewed his job" in Paris, Strether muses in the London theater, "it was 'types' he should have to tackle" in Europe

(*TA* 44). Strether is an incomplete frame, a potential but as yet unattached ill-detachable detachment, but he becomes aware in Europe of the emptiness at the center of his life:

> There were sequences he had missed and great gaps in the procession: he might have been watching it all recede in a golden cloud of dust. If the playhouse wasn't closed his seat had at least fallen to somebody else. (*TA* 64)

Though he fears it may be too late, he takes refuge in this new aesthetic, his only chance for salvation in "the great desert of years" (*TA* 63), and he sets out "to visit unattended equivocal performances" (*TA* 64).

Strether's ideal is the mystical aesthetic of Paris, and his espousal of it is a reaction against the crude good-and-bad, right-and-wrong morality of Woollett. Strether describes himself as "'a perfectly equipped failure'" (*TA* 40), but the fact that he is a failure is what makes Strether so interesting to Maria Gostrey, whose function in the story is to enunciate this aesthetic, "the shade of shyness" (*TA* 96), that Strether must discover through his experience in Europe:

> "Thank goodness you're a failure—it's why I so distinguish you. Anything else to-day is too hideous. Look about you—look at the successes. Would you *be* one, on your honor?" (*TA* 40).

Julie Rivkin shows that Miss Gostrey "deconstructs the literal system of designation Woollett supposedly embodies" (826) in order to introduce Strether to the European system, and her use of the term "deconstruct" clarifies the sense in which the Paris aesthetic and the Woollett ethic are diametrically and dialectically opposed.[6] The aesthetic of Paris prefers failure to success, and it is appealing to the "man of imagination" (*TA* 5) from Woollett because he is himself a failure. Paris offers him a chance to revel in his failure instead of compensating for it by marrying Mrs. Newsome. It offers him, therefore, a new light in which to view the memories of his youth, and it has the effect of making him feel young again.

The Paris aesthetic prefers failure to success because of a more fundamental preference of potential to action. This principle, reminiscent of Gabriel Nash, is exemplified by the peculiar beauty of little Bilham and enunciated again by Miss Gostrey:

> "The others have all wanted so dreadfully to do something, and they've gone and done it too in many cases indeed. It leaves them never the same afterwards; the charm's always somehow broken. Now *he*, I think, you know, really won't. He won't do the least dreadful little thing. We shall continue to enjoy him just as he is. No—he's quite beautiful. He sees everything. He isn't a bit

> ashamed. He has every scrap of the courage of it that one could ask. Only think what he *might* do." (*TA* 87)

Unlike Miriam Rooth, Little Bilham is an artist whose "productive power faltered in proportion as his knowledge grew" (*TA* 84), and he is "beautiful" in his inactivity. He is the perfect product of the Paris aesthetic: Bilham is "'the best of them,'" "'so exactly right as he is'" (*TA* 86). Strether soon learns that "almost any acceptance of Paris might give one's authority away" (*TA* 64)—one's authority, that is, to do anything at all. Paris is not a place of action or of power but a place where people are simply and statically "wonderful." Toward the end of the novel, at the point where Strether is most oppressed by the weight of the Paris aesthetic, he recalls wistfully the full import of his "'Don't mention it!'" to Madame de Vionnet:

> it had served all the purpose of his appearing to have said to her: "Don't like me, if it's a question of liking me, for anything obvious and clumsy that I've, as they call it, 'done' for you: like me—well, like me, hang it, for anything else you choose. . . . Be for me, please, with all your admirable tact and trust, just whatever I may show you it's a present pleasure to me to think you." It had been a large indication to meet; but if she hadn't met it what *had* she done, and how had their time together slipped along so smoothly, mild but not slow, and melting, liquefying, into his happy illusion of idleness? (*TA* 304-05)

The emphasis here is clearly on being rather than doing and on pleasure rather than sincerity. The Paris aesthetic, in short, supplies Strether with this "happy illusion of idleness," the illusion that he is doing nothing and having no effect on the people around him. Though Strether remains determined in the early chapters of the novel to carry out his orders from Woollett and to play his role as emissary, he comes to expect much more than Chad's acquiescence from his trip to Europe. He embarks alone on a conscious search for his ideal, and he knows that to find truth he will have to get rid of his "odious ascetic suspicion of any form of beauty" (*TA* 118).

The journey to primacy Strether embarks on in Paris takes the form of a romantic quest for the ideal at Gloriani's party. In Gloriani's garden Strether opens "all the windows of his mind" to the "assault of images" that crowns the great sculptor "with the light, with the romance, of glory" (*TA* 120). Strether perceives himself to be on trial in this scene, seeing Gloriani's smile as "a test of his stuff" (*TA* 121). Strether's ideal is youth, and his tribute to this ideal, his promise to "save" Madame de Vionnet (*TA* 152), is the foundation of his quest. Strether is absorbed into the drama of the garden, and his mode of perception blurs almost imperceptibly from the dramatic to the romantic. In *Anatomy of Criticism*, Northrop Frye writes that romance involves an adventure, often a quest, and an enemy "associated with winter, darkness, confusion, sterility, moribund life, and old age," while the hero is conversely associated with "spring, dawn, fertility, vigor, and youth" (Frye 187-88). A romance, Frye writes, is a myth in which the hero is human, not divine (Frye 188), and its culmination is "the victory of fertility over the wasteland" (Frye 193). My purpose is not to claim that *The Ambassadors* is a romance ("Subtlety and complexity are not much favored," Frye writes, and "irony has little place in a romance" [Frye 195]) but to show that Strether has begun to perceive his role in the story as that of a romantic hero. Gloriani, crowned "with the light, with the romance, of glory," is the feudal king and Strether, the knight who must prove himself, sets off on a quest. The goal of Strether's romantic quest is Madame de Vionnet, the spectacular *femme du monde*:

> This [the *femmes du monde*] was a category our friend had a feeling for; a light, romantic and mysterious, on the feminine element, in which he enjoyed for a little watching it. (*TA* 122)

Strether is from Woollett and he knows what it means when a man and a woman involve themselves in a relationship. What he knows, exactly, is that unless such a relationship is legitimized by legal union it is bad, but Strether's quest is for the fairy queen, the only woman with whom the term "virtuous attachment" would not necessarily be a euphemism. He ignores Bilham's hint that the relationship may not be as virtuous as he imagines:

> Strether came round to it. "They then are the virtuous attachment?"
>
> "I can only tell you it's what they pass for. But isn't that enough? What more than a vain appearance does the wisest of us know? I commend you," the young man declared with a pleasant emphasis, "the vain appearance."
>
> (*TA* 124)

He ignores this obviously prophetic warning because life in Paris is a romance to Strether. No element of the great city inspires him more to wax romantic than Madame de Vionnet, and his quest is to rescue this *femme du monde* from Chad, the "brute" (*TA* 335):

> he found himself making out, as a background of the occupant [Madame de Vionnet], some glory, some prosperity of the First Empire, some Napoleonic glamour, some dim lustre of the great legend; elements clinging still to all the consular chairs and mythological brasses and sphinxes' heads and faded surfaces of satin striped with alternate silk. (*TA* 145)

She is the object of his quest because of what she represents; with her "air of youth" (*TA* 127) she embodies his ideal, and his promise to save her becomes his "constant tribute to the ideal" (*TA* 241), the aesthetic ideal that Christof Wegelin calls "social beauty" (Wegelin 442). But the climax of the novel comes not when he rescues Madame de Vionnet but when he discovers the true nature of their attachment, framed as it is by Jeanne, and the extent to which he has been fooled by the romance of Paris.

Much attention has been paid to the viscosity of imagery in *The Ambassadors*. James Wise shows that Strether is "a man floating between two mental reactions without a center of self-knowledge or self-reliance on which to build a foundation for decision" (Wise 84). Wise concludes that Strether alternates in the novel "between a series of risings and plungings" (Wise 109) and that he escapes from the Woollett morality and floats off alone at the end. Reginald Abbott, more recently, has shown that the floating imagery that dominates *The Ambassadors* implies a reversal of the iconographical gender roles of fin-de-siècle culture, in which floating and inactivity were associated with the feminine while flying and activity were male attributes. Both these readings conclude that the water imagery in *The Ambassadors* is an expression of Strether's passivity, a conclusion supported by the ambivalent last line of the novel and by the way Strether seems now to be in one boat, now in another, and now floating randomly or washed up on some shore.[7] These critics, however, have overlooked the one event in which Strether acts on his own initiative, changing drastically the course of future events. This unique and isolated action in Chapter 31 stands out both from the general fluidity of the novel and from the dream-like romance of the chapter itself as the climax or "*peripeteia*" (Lodge 208) of the book. Some have read the Lambinet chapters of *The Ambassadors* as Strether's descent into self deception.[8] I will argue, though, that the Lambinet chapters at the same time portray Strether's greatest triumph of the novel, for it is here that Strether finally breaks free of the destructive Paris aesthetic.

Lambert Strether's break for freedom from Woollett begins as soon as he steps off the boat in Chester, but it is not finalized until the end of Chapter 27, and then quite by accident. Strether has vowed that whatever happens in Paris he will get nothing for himself: "it was to an ideal rigour that he had quite promised himself to conform" (*TA* 201). He realizes that by living his ideal he has separated himself from the rest of the world, and he is conscious of this separation:

> His danger, at any rate, . . . was some concession, . . . that would involve a sharp rupture with the actual; therefore if he waited to take leave of that actual he might wholly miss his chance. (*TA* 201)

The "actual" referred to here is America, of which Strether himself is the representative until he is replaced by Sarah. Sarah represents the corporeality of human nature, which the Pococks have come to curtail with their staunch morality, and Madame de Vionnet represents an alternative to that morality. When Strether shifts from "the rigors of New England authority to the pleasures of Parisian experience" (Rivkin 827), Sarah Pocock replaces him as ambassador of the actual, leaving him in limbo, and Strether's "rupture with the actual" is finalized at the end of Chapter 27, when Strether's break with Sarah is complete:

> The way he had put it to himself was that all quite *might* be at an end. Each of her movements, in this resolute rupture, reaffirmed, re-enforced that idea. Sarah passed out of sight in the sunny street while, planted there in the centre of the comparatively grey court, he continued merely to look before him. It probably *was* all at an end. (*TA* 280)

But Strether, always patient, still drags his feet, taking time for extended interviews with Chad and Miss Gostrey before acknowledging this rupture with action.

At the end of Chapter 29 there is a significant break in the action like that which obfuscates Isabel's marriage in *The Portrait of a Lady*, and when the next chapter begins a change seems to have taken place both in Strether and in the tone of the narration. Robert Garis writes that after "twenty-nine chapters dramatizing, with extraordinarily close attention to the rigors of a consistent point of view" the book ends with seven chapters in which "the writing is brilliant in invention and secure in justice" (309-10). We are denied all details of Strether's decision to leave Paris for the day, and we see him only as his train approaches the station where he will disembark and begin his adventure. The break is heightened by one of James's enigmatic shifts into past-perfect narration, a shift that, like the past perfect at the beginning of the governess's narrative in *The Turn of the Screw,* indicates the passage of time and compensates for the lack of a beginning to the episode.

> [Strether] had taken the train a few days after this from a station—as well as to a station—selected almost at random; such days, whatever should happen, were numbered, and he had gone forth under the impulse—artless enough, no doubt—to give the whole of one of them to that French ruralism, with its cool special green, into which he had hitherto looked only through the little oblong window of the picture-frame. (*TA* 300-01)

A threshold has clearly been crossed during the break: a gap has somehow been somehow left unbridged, and Strether is entering a realm that has always been distant from him and sacred. He has decided to devote a day to

> that French Ruralism, with its cool special green, into which he had hitherto looked only through the little oblong window of the picture-frame. It had been as yet for the most part but a land of fancy for him—the background of fiction, the medium of art, the nursery of letters; practically as distant as Greece, but practically also well-nigh as consecrated. (*TA* 301)

Strether has broken with both Paris and Woollett, transcending the dialectical quagmire of thesis and antithesis. His train journey is not so much to a place as to a realm of his remembered past that he has neglected since the time when he nearly bought a Lambinet painting as a young man. His memory of the painting becomes his ideal, and he goes to the countryside to reconstruct it:

> he could thrill a little at the chance of seeing something somewhere that would remind him of a certain small Lambinet that had charmed him, long years before, at a Boston dealer's and that he had quite absurdly never forgotten. (*TA* 301)

Strether is yearning in wishful regret, but not for the painting itself that he decided not to buy in Boston: "he never found himself wishing that the wheel of time would turn it up again." He wants to breathe life into the memory of the painting, to live and experience it as he could have done when he was young. His longing is not for the painting itself but for what it meant for him: "He wasn't there to dip, to consume—he was there to reconstruct" (*TA* 67). Strether pursues this reconstruction of his youth actively in Chapter 30: "it would be a different thing, however, to see the remembered mixture resolved back into its elements—to assist at the restoration of the whole far-away hour" (*TA* 301). His adventure at the gallery had been a "modest" one (*TA* 301), but his memory of the picture has "made him for a moment overstep the modesty of nature" (*TA* 301) by trying to reconstruct the work of art in its place of origin. It is this quest to recover his ideal, the feelings of one of the few adventures of his youth, and to experience those feelings again, that has motivated Strether's excursion into the country and "French Ruralism."

On his journey out of dusty Paris Strether's memory of the painting continues to dominate his perception of the world, and he views the French countryside as a painting framed by the window of the train:

> The oblong gilt frame disposed its enclosing lines; the poplars and willows, the reeds and river—a river of which he didn't know, and didn't want to know, the name—fell into a composition, full of felicity, within them; the sky was silver

> and turquoise and varnish; the village on the left was white and the church on the right was grey; it was all there, in short—it was what he wanted. (*TA* 302)

When he arrives at the station Strether leaves the train, in effect, through this window, stepping into the tone and texture of the painting of his youth. What he finds as he steps into "French ruralism," into his memory of a Lambinet painting he "*would* have bought" (*TA* 301) is "the colors of life itself" (*LC* 65). He is absorbed by a world that is no less surreal than Maisie's in the Fairy Tale sequence.

What has happened, ironically, is that Strether has been released from the bounds of fictionality: he has stepped out of the painting and into the frame. Equally detached now from ethic and aesthetic, he is free to reconstruct the world as he chooses. Strether's idealization of the world continues throughout the day:

> [He] had admired, had almost coveted, another small old church, all steep roof and dim slate-colour without and all whitewash and paper flowers within; had lost his way and had found it again; had conversed with rustics who struck him perhaps a little more as men of the world than he had expected; had acquired at a bound a fearless facility in French; had had, as the afternoon waned, a watery bock, all pale and Parisian, in the café of the furthest village, which was not the biggest; and had meanwhile not once overstepped the oblong gilt frame. . . . It might have passed for finished, his drama, with its catastrophe all but reached: it had, however, none the less been vivid again for him as he thus gave it its fuller chance. He had only had to be at last well out of it to feel it, oddly enough, still going on. (*TA* 305)

What James calls in the Preface the dialectical "drama of discrimination" (*TA* 7), Strether realizes, has been going on without him since the arrival of the Pococks, and his response is to step out of it into the audience, where he notices that his absence from the stage is hardly missed. Strether's drama, he realizes, is larger and more beautiful than he has ever imagined, and it continues to expand and open up for him. This epiphanic discovery, a sudden release of the pressure Strether has been under since he arrived in Europe, is exhilarating to him, and he sits back in euphoric detachment to watch the drama of the world happen in front of him:

> it was all there, in short; it was what he wanted: it was Tremont Street, it was France, it was Lambinet. Moreover, he was freely walking about in it. (*TA* 302)

Strether's detachment from the world is no longer merely the reminder of his failure that it has always been, "the period of conscious detachment occupying the centre of his life, the grey desert of the two deaths, that of his wife and that, ten years later, of his boy" (*TA* 43). It has become his moment of triumph. Strether's new world, where there is "not a breath of the cooler evening that wasn't somehow a syllable of the text" (*TA* 306), nears consistency and completeness as he steps away from it, and the people performing on Strether's stage are "inevitable," "natural," and "right" (*TA* 306). He discovers that

> it was essentially more than anything else a scene and a stage, that the very air of the play was in the rustle of the willows and the tone of the sky. The play and the characters had, without his knowing it till now, peopled all his space for him. . . . (*TA* 306)

The bounds of the story, its plot and the relations between its characters, have somehow dissolved, leaving Strether in a dream fantasy, wandering about the countryside and seeing everything just as he would like it to be. He is in a world made entirely of his own impressions, a drama nearly complete and perfect. The drama Strether has been watching unfold before him reaches its catastrophe at the end of Chapter 30, by which point Strether is so pleased with the vista and with his day in the countryside that he requires only a "comfortable climax" (*TA* 306):

> the confidence that had so gathered for him deepened with the lap of the water, the ripple of the surface, the rustle of the reeds on the opposite bank, the faint diffused coolness, and the slight rock of a couple of small boats attached to a rough landing-place hard by. (*TA* 307)

When Strether is absorbed by the frame, the story briefly becomes Strether's autobiography[9] as he repays the debt he owes himself for not buying the Lambinet in his youth. In effect, he is re-writing his life by trying to find in art what he has missed in reality. The narrator is still present, perhaps more so than ever, but we are allowed to see what the story would have been like if Strether were the narrator: a romance, predictably composed and tinctured with idealism, and with a happy ending.

Leon Edel has written that *The Turn of the Screw* must be read as two different stories, one of the governess's fancy and one of fact (Edel 233). This must, of course, be true of any novel where a center of consciousness is the narrative vehicle. The point of Strether's quest in *The Ambassadors* is that these two stories must converge: Lambert Strether, in other words, must match his imagination with the world around him. The fanciful story is the immediate one that I have been describing, Strether's wishful romanticization, but the factual story, is the one we read, in which Strether charges with the momentum of a speeding train toward a reunion with the actual with which he has ruptured, and this forms the climax of the novel: the two stories converge at the point where they are most divergent. We have long detected hints as to the nature of the relationship between Chad and Madame de Vionnet, the most obvious of which is Strether's discovery in Chapter 19 that they are both mysteriously "out of town" (*TA* 200) at the same time, but Strether is oblivious to these hints. There is no suspense at all in Strether's version of the outing, but in ours there is no sure indication that Strether will survive the crash we know is imminent. When Strether sees the man and the woman in the boat his constructed picture/drama is complete, and his satisfaction with his impressions rivals James's own in the Preface:[10]

> It was as if these figures, or something like them, had been wanted in the picture, had been wanted more or less all day, and had now drifted into sight, with the slow current, on purpose to fill up the measure. (*TA* 307)[11]

As we know, Strether is about to discover that he knows the two figures in the boat, and that there are things he has hitherto not known about the romance he has left behind in Paris.

The dissolution of the fictional bounds of the story and the absorption into the oblong gilt frame are more than an indication that Strether is deceiving himself, though he surely is. The lapse in time before Chapter 30, the past-perfect narration, and the lyrical and pastoral tone in that chapter all seem to indicate that the frame through which Strether has passed is no mere metaphor. He has passed, more literally than we first imagine, into a new realm of being. Strether is overcome with the charm of the drama around him because he has transcended it. He has been absorbed through the frame into the painting he saw in Boston and is able to thrill to the lush texture of the world because he is detached from it, but at the same time he has transcended his own story, and this fact raises a question: if Strether is in the book but not in the story, where exactly is he? He is observing the world, looking at it as a detached and disinterested connoisseur because he is in the frame of the story. Strether jumps, in fact, from his story to ours in the Lambinet chapter. He leaves his post as fictional hero and steps back to read his own story as it unfolds from a detached vantage point. Fact and fancy are related to each other like work and frame or, more specifically and more pertinently to the work of Henry James, like novel and preface. The preface to a book is the place where the author releases himself from all pretext of fiction and explains his intention, and there is nothing but tradition to dictate that the preface must be printed at the beginning—as Derrida notes in *Dissemination* (1972),

> Time is the time of the preface; space—whose time *will have been* the Truth—is the space of the preface. The preface would thus occupy the entire *location* and *duration* of the book. (*D* 13)

As Strether views the world through the oblong frame of the window of the train and is thus absorbed into his memory of the painting he unwittingly enters the frame of his own story and finds himself on the outside looking in. Strether has long played the role of the aesthete, viewing his friends as paintings in a gallery and actors on a stage, and his imagination carries him in Chapter 30 into the frame itself, where he can look down on the rest of the world with the detachment of the Joycean creator, "paring his fingernails." It is only from this new vantage point, virtually our own vantage point, that Strether is able to see the true nature of the "virtuous attachment." The mechanics of this framing episode are crucial to an understanding of the novel.

The frame exists, as we have seen, beside the work, redressing a lack that cannot be eliminated within the work itself, thus providing external completeness. But the nature of this completeness is problematic and needs to be clarified. In *Dissemination*, in the propaedutic essay entitled "Outwork," Derrida explores the function of the preface to a book, which I think is relevant here. He invokes the ancient metaphor of the world, our world as we see it, as a final and divine text that imitates nature, a text that all other texts aspire to imitate. A book, then, in the tradition of western metaphysics, cannot imitate nature directly and must instead imitate or preface the world, which is itself also a text. But a text itself can never be complete or all-encompassing, and a frame is thus not an arbitrary attachment but a necessary one. If the world is a text, this implies

> that nature is somewhere incomplete, that it lacks something needed for it to be what it is, that it has to be supplemented. . . . The book comes to add itself to nature . . . , but through this addition it must also complete nature, fulfill its essence. (*D* 53)

The book, which imitates the world, becomes a preface or frame to the world, imitating nature by redressing some incompleteness in it. But the book, which aims to complete the world by prefacing it, is itself incomplete: literature, then, like the world,

> seems to aim toward the filling of a lack (a hole) in a whole that should not itself in its essence be missing (to) itself. But literature is also the *exception to everything*: at once the exception to the whole, the want-of-wholeness in the whole, and the exception to everything, that which exists by itself, alone, with

nothing else, in exception to all. A part that, within *and* without the whole, marks the wholly other, the other incommensurate with the whole. (*D* 56)

Like nature, literature is completed not by an alteration that would eliminate the lack (the nature analogy illustrates the futility of such an attempt) but by juxtaposition with something else. The lack is not merely eliminated but made into a positive element instead of a negative one: it is thus that in "Parergon" Derrida answers the question of why a column of a building and a garment worn by a figure in a painting are parerga:

> It is not because they are detached but on the contrary because they are so difficult to detach and above all because without them, without their quasi-detachment, the lack on the inside of the work would appear; or (which amounts to the same thing for a lack) would not appear. (*TP* 59)

The world prefaces nature, the book prefaces the world, and the preface, in the same way and for the same reasons, frames the book. In a work of art the issue is not whether or not the lack appears in the work (completeness is an impossible aim) but whether it contributes to the work or detracts from it. The lack is transformed by the parergon from a negative absence to a positive one, just as Mrs. Newsome's poor health is transformed by Strether into an omnipotence that is felt throughout the novel. I invoke Derrida here again because his work illustrates how the book is less an autonomous whole than a preface to another text. The book thus bears a greater resemblance to its own preface than to itself, and my thesis, that Chapters 30 and 31 of *The Ambassadors* in effect form a preface to the work, is an extension of Derrida's argument into the realm of fiction.

We must isolate the lack in the work that would necessitate such a preface. Rivkin, who reads *The Ambassadors* in terms of Derrida's logic of the supplement, mentions the lack in her explanation but makes no attempt to isolate any fundamental lack in the novel that might necessitate supplementation. The most obvious lack at the center of *The Ambassadors*, of course, is the truth, the nature of the "virtuous attachment," to which we as readers are privy but Strether is blind for much of the novel. Strether searches for the truth of the virtuous attachment, never finding it but drawing ever closer with graceful diligence, but Strether's convergence upon his asymptotic ideal would violate the rigor of realism: he is an elderly man from Woollett, Massachusetts, and it would simply not be realistic for him to achieve a full understanding of his place in the world within the context of the story. The Lambinet scene is a revelation, but a revelation is something we interpret, not a discrete literal message disclosing the answer to a problem. The truth has no place in a realistic text, but at the same time it is unavoidable here because the subject of the portrait, Lambert Strether, is in search of the truth. Strether's nature as a "man of imagination" necessitates the truth, but a realistic portrait forbids its encroachment upon the unity of the composition. In a sense, then, the lack is the truth, and since this truth must be both present to and detached from the work, it must be disclosed in a frame. The chapters can be called a preface because they disclose, in a completely different style and mode than the rest of the novel, a truth that cannot be expressed in the work but must be expressed of the work. This truth, like those truths that fill the prefaces in *The Art of the Novel*, can only exist in exclusion.

But there is another more fundamental lack in the text that is redressed in Chapter 31 as an effect of this disclosure of truth: it is the lack of action. This inaction is the main premise of the Paris aesthetic I have described above. Action is vulgar under the Paris aesthetic, and beauty is found in one's potential, not one's endeavors. Action is what makes Waymarsh so increasingly unappealing to Strether as he wanders deeper into Parisian culture. All action in Strether's Paris is performance, which, like sacrifice, is action that merely pays tribute to an ideal. The only real action in the novel before the Lambinet chapters is Strether's "'Live all you can; it's a mistake not to'" speech (*TA* 132), and even this action is a passive and pitiful one. The speech, which has been taken by many critics of *The Ambassadors* (including, at least ostensibly, James himself at the beginning of the Preface) at its face value, is actually evidence of how confused Strether is by the party in Gloriani's garden. He tells little Bilham,

> "It doesn't so much matter what you do in particular, so long as you have your life. If you haven't had that, what *have* you had? This place and these impressions—mild as you may find them to wind a man up so; all my impressions of Chad and of people I've seen at *his* place—well, have had their abundant message for me. I see it now. I haven't done so before—and now I'm old; too old at any rate for what I see. Oh I *do* see, at least; and more than you'd believe or I can express. It's too late. And it's as if the train had fairly waited at the station for me without my having had the gumption to know it was there." (*TA* 132)

Strether's message is clearly that he can see now what he should have done when he was young and that Bilham must do things now before he is too old to do anything at all. Bilham naturally assumes that it is Gloriani whom Strether "should enjoy being like" (TA 133) because Gloriani is a successful artist, but Strether is dazzled by Gloriani more because he is successful than because he is an artist—Gloriani has lived. Strether's message is misinterpreted by Bilham, the Paris aesthete who seems to have heard not "live all you can" but "see all you can":

> "Didn't you adjure me, in accents I shall never forget, to see, while I've a chance, everything I can?—and *really* to see, for it must have been that only you meant." (*TA* 165)

With the exception of the "'Live all you can'" speech, the novel is virtually devoid of action on Strether's part, and this, his only action before Chapter 31, is less an action than a sentimental speech about action, and one that is interpreted to be a speech about inaction. The Paris aesthetic is a morass of passivity and an abyss of inactivity, and this speech is its low point; it is here, though he does not see it, that Strether touches bottom.

The only action of the novel, the only event that would necessitate a transitive verb in a summary of the plot, comes at the beginning of Chapter 31. When Strether realizes that Chad and Madame de Vionnet are in the boat below him, he sees that "what it all came to had been that fiction and fable *were*, inevitably, in the air" (*TA* 311). He is able to see that his friends have been withholding details from him because he has stepped out of the story, as they have, and has surprised them out of costume. The catastrophe, the revelation to Strether of the identities of the boaters, is "a sharp fantastic crisis that had popped up as if in a dream" (*TA* 308), and Strether's realization puts him in command for the first time in the novel, perhaps for the first time in his life. Knowing that the others are not sure whether he has recognized them, he has the power to decide the future of his relationship with Chad and Madame de Vionnet. From his new vantage point he is able to decide either to be absorbed into the aesthetic of Paris or to repudiate it, and he must make his choice in seconds. If he decides to play the game of Paris by pretending not to have seen them, i.e., by doing nothing, he will possess a secret about them and will be able to observe their attempts to disguise what he knows now to be the truth about their relationship. This alternative might seem a tempting one to a man whose confidence has been used as Strether's has, but he refuses this opportunity for power, choosing instead the honest, jovial, and extravagant wave of recognition:

> He hereupon gave large play to [surprise and joy], agitating his hat and his stick and loudly calling out—a demonstration that brought him relief as soon as he had seen it answered. (*TA* 308)

The symbolic sexuality latent in this stick-waving climax, symbolic of the most primitive action of all, is clearly proof that he has now renounced the metaphysical and returned, at least partially, to the actual. David

Lodge has pointed out that the plethora of water imagery throughout the novel is "ironically prophetic" (Lodge 205):

> How appropriate it is . . . that Strether, at the climax of an experience which he has consistently likened to swimming in or navigating a watery medium, at the very point where he has to reassess this experience and acknowledge the partial correctness of the Woollett interpretation of events, should be returned to the Woollett stance on the shore and recognize the deviousness of Chad's and Madame de Vionnet's conduct, as they come drifting down the river in a boat. (Lodge 208)

Drama, of course, is action, and Strether, no longer Mrs. Newsome's proxy, begins here to act on his own. It is ironic that Strether does not act in the drama until he has stepped out of it. The rest of Chapter 31 is the denouement of the drama, Strether's descent back to the work and the world in which he belongs.

The Lambinet chapters form a frame because they contain the truth and the action that must be excluded from the text. The frame of a painting generally jumps forward and forces both figure and ground into the background while fading out of sight when one looks intently at the inside of the work, but a peculiarity of this frame is that though it easily jumps forward into primacy it has a hard time fading away, and the reason for this is that this frame contains the climax of the book: to say that the novel lacks truth and action is simply a delicate way of saying that it lacks a climax and must lack one, hence its relegation to the frame. One question raised by James's text is also answered by this exclusion: what do we make of James's propriety in relying so heavily on chance at such a crucial point? The coincidence of Strether's journeying to the same village that his friends are using for their retreat is only partially explained away by its ironic appropriateness. Unnatural coincidence, like truth and action, has no place in a novelistic portrait even of an imaginative man in Paris, but like them also this unnatural coincidence is no obstacle in a preface, where the author simply explains what he meant and how it happened under no obligation to conform to nature. James's exclusion of the climax, the great floating revelation, from the rest of the work has led Mary Ann Caws to read the recognition wrongly as an anticlimax (Caws 157). James's intensification of the frame makes it vie for prominence with the work itself, this paralleling Strether's own progress toward primacy.

After his initial action, which so alters the course of future events, Strether coolly and elegantly reverts to his old idle ways, playing along with the lie and "superseding mere violence" (*TA* 308):

> It had been a performance, Madame de Vionnet's manner, and though it had to that degree faltered toward the end, as through her ceasing to believe in it, as if she had asked herself, or Chad had found a moment surreptitiously to ask her, what after all was the use, a performance it had none the less quite handsomely remained, with the final fact about it that it was on the whole easier to keep up than to abandon. (*TA* 311)

Strether has left the oblong gilt frame behind now and has re-entered the drama of Paris as an active participant, an entity now to be reckoned with. The difference is that Strether now knows, as the others do, that he is acting in a drama, a fiction in which everyone has, like Chad and Madame de Vionnet, "something to put a face upon" (*TA* 310). No longer an acolyte of one branch of a dialectic or the other, "He was, at that point of vantage, in full possession, to make of it all what he could" (*TA* 311). Strether learns from his adventure in the countryside that he has always been more than a proxy to Mrs. Newsome, that he is involved in the drama and has always been, and that he has been fooled. Though there can be no absolute knowledge or revelation within realism, there can and must be understanding through impression and imagination:

> [Strether] realized at last that he had really been trying all along to suppose nothing. Verily, verily, his labour had been lost. He found himself supposing innumerable and wonderful things. (*TA* 313)

On the basis of his discovery of the lie and his realization of its truth Strether repudiates Maria Gostrey in much the same way that Maisie renounces Mrs Beale and Sir Claude, and he begins, in the last pages of the novel, to find himself. Renunciation, in James, is often a step toward maturity, and it is a skill that both Maisie and Strether ultimately acquire.

Strether's real discovery, though, is not so much the nature of the virtuous attachment itself as the fact that "his [own] moral superiority has vanished" (Wegelin 449) and that he is himself "mixed up with the typical tale of Paris" (*TA* 315). In the *Postes et Télégraphs* Strether notes that there is

> something in the air of these establishments; the vibration of the vast strange life of the town, the influence of the types, the performers concocting their messages; the little prompt Paris women, arranging, pretexting goodness knew what, driving the dreadful needle-pointed pen at the dreadful sand-strewn public table. . . . He was mixed up with the typical tale of Paris, and so were they, poor things—how could they altogether help being? (*TA* 314-15)

Strether has slowly come to realize a profound truth: that he has been involved all along in the drama and that behind the veil of the aesthetic of Paris are real people, all of whom are also actively participating in the drama of life, as Chad and Madame de Vionnet have been behind his back. He also sees, of course, that "somebody was paying something somewhere and somehow, that they were at least not all floating together on the silver stream of impunity" (*TA* 315), and he understandably reverts for a time to the "old tradition" (*TA* 316) of the Woollett morality, "the notion that the state of the wrongdoer, or at least this person's happiness, presented some special difficulty" (*TA* 316). Strether goes to see Maria Gostrey for one last time, however, and "As she presented things the ugliness—goodness knew why—went out of them" and Strether's indignant anger begins to subside. He sees how much his naivete has aided his friends' intimacy, and he comes slowly, and indeed miraculously, to see this intimacy as a positive thing. "'What it comes to,'" he explains to Miss Gostrey, "'is that it's not, that it's never, a happiness, any happiness at all, to *take*. The only safe thing is to give. It's what plays you least false'" (*TA* 321). This maxim in Strether's enlightened grasp is no mere cliché: its profundity is evidenced by "the quaver of [Maria's] quietness" (*TA* 321) as she takes it in.

In his excursion to the frame Strether renounces both Woollett and Paris, but in the end he takes upon himself the task of combining the Woollett ethic and the Paris aesthetic, thus reconciling thesis and antithesis with synthesis. The end result of *The Ambassadors*, the mysterious "product" produced at Woollett and refined in Paris, is Lambert Strether, a man who sees both the crudity and the validity of the culture he was born into. But he also sees both the beauty and the hypocrisy of the Parisian culture. In short, he has educated himself: midway through the novel he could barely "'toddle alone'" (*TA* 190), but at the end he has learned from his adventures that the view of Paris as the "consecrated scene of rash infatuations and bold bad treacheries" belongs to the infancy of life as well as of art.[12] Strether has retained the broad view of life afforded by his trip to Europe and his adventure in the preface and has grown out of that infancy. His successful mediation between Woollett and Paris is what earns him the title of ambassador.

NOTES

NOTES TO THE PREFACE

[1] For an analysis of the debate between Besant and James, see Mark Spilka's "'The Art of Fiction' Controversy."

[2] See "Economimesis," in which Derrida argues that the frame of Kant's third *Critique* is vomit.

[3] See, for example, Derrida's recent essay on the European identity, "The Other Heading: Memories, Responses, and Responsibilities," in which he argues that

> *what is proper to a culture is not to be identical to itself.* Not to not have an identity, but to be able to identify itself, to be able to say "me" or "we"; to be able to take the form of a subject only in the non-identity to itself or, if you prefer, only in the difference with itself. There is no culture or cultural identity without this difference *with itself.* (p. 90)

[4] I will use the word "redress" here because the action to which I refer is not that of eliminating the lack but of compensating for it. "Redress," as a transitive verb, is a more forceful and dominating verb than "compensate" and thus better approximates the action of the parergon.

NOTES TO CHAPTER I

[1] *TP* 125.

[2] See the Preface to *The Portrait of a Lady* for James's explication of the theory of central consciousness narration.

[3] I borrow the concept of "objecthood" from Michael Fried's essay "Art and Objecthood." Fried's position, that art that emphasizes its own objecthood is theatrical, is clearly supported by my reading of *The Tragic Muse,* in which Miriam transcends her objecthood and develops from an object of the theater into a work of modernist realism.

[4] In the first chapter James's characters are aesthetically impotent—Nick, the best among them, is only a bad artist, a "duffer" (*TM* 20). In fact, Nick Dormer is nothing at all when the story begins, and the question Biddy and Miriam later address is what, if anything, he will become (a question that is never fully resolved):

> "If your brother's an artist, I don't understand how he's in Parliament."
> "Oh, he isn't in Parliament now; we only hope he will be."
> "Oh, I see."
> "And he isn't an artist, either," Biddy felt herself conscientiously bound to subjoin.

> "Then he isn't anything," said Miss Rooth.
> "Well—he's immensely clever."
> "Oh, I see," Miss Rooth again replied. (*TM* 116)

Nick is nothing from Miriam's point of view because he has done nothing, which in turn is because he has not yet made the choice between art and life. The distinction between art and life is blurred, then, to emphasize the void in the beginning of the novel of both substance and action—in fact, it is done to obscure the very existence of the characters, to make them ghosts.

[5] See Goetz, "The Allegory of Representation in *The Tragic Muse,*" for the puns on the word "representation" in the novel.

[6] They seem at first to subscribe to the aesthetic model by Lady Agnes as it is summarized by her son Nick:

> "She has inherited the queer old superstition that art is pardonable only so long as it is bad—so long as it's done at odd hours, for a little distraction, like a game of tennis or whist. The only thing that can justify it, the effort to carry it as far as one can (which you can't do without time and singleness of purpose), she regards as just the dangerous, the criminal element. It's the oddest hind-part-before view, the drollest immorality." (*TM* 19)

Lady Agnes wants nothing to do with art and is suspicious of it, but although she is rendered satirically her view of art is taken seriously in the novel. Julia Dallow, also, hates art (*TM* 343).

[7] The early chapters of the novel are built on a series of "*alternation*[s]" (*AN* 90) or oppositions, and these oppositions are always shifting, forming what Meir Sternberg calls a "dance-like movement" (Sternberg 801) about the center. Sternberg shows that in *The Tragic Muse* James "moves the center of gravity from temporal process towards spatial configuration" (Sternberg 785) and notes the appropriateness of this scheme to a novel about an actress:

> since [Miriam Rooth] is conceived of as the quintessential actress off as well as on stage, it is appropriate that she should be projected in terms of the effects and impressions she produces on other observers. (Sternberg 755)

[8] This, of course, is the traditional role of a muse:

> Thus great with child to speak, and helpless in my throes,
> Biting my truant pen, beating myself for spite:
> "Fool!" said my muse to me, "look in thy heart, and write."
> Sir Philip Sidney, *Astrophel and Stella,* Sonnet 1.

[9] As with my citations from James, all italics and parentheses are Kant's own. Square brackets are Pulhar's, and I have retained in my transcriptions only those of Pulhar's bracketed additions to the text whose absence would interrupt the flow of the translation.

[10] See Kant, §17 and §34. See also Derrida: "examples are the wheelchairs of judgement" (*TP* 79).

[11] Heidegger writes:

> On the usual view, the work arises out of and by means of the activity of the artist. But by what and whence is the artist what he is? By the work; for to say that the work does credit to the master means that it is the work that lets the artist

emerge as a master of his art. The artist is the origin of the work. The work is the origin of the artist. Neither is without the other. (Heidegger 17)

[12] Nietzsche may have Kant in mind when he complains that

> Our aesthetics hitherto has been a woman's aesthetics to the extent that only the receivers of art have formulated their experience of "what is beautiful?" In all philosophy hitherto the artist is lacking—. (*The Will to Power* #811)

See *Spurs* 77 for Derrida's discussion of this text.

[13] Kant portrays a world similar to that in which James's novel begins, concentrating on the object and the subject and rarely mentioning the artist or artistic method: "in fine art there is only *manner* (*modus*), not *method* (*methodus*)" (Kant 230). For Kant on perfection in fine art, see §48.

[14] See Litvak's essay, which links the admirable with drama and the detestable with the theater and notes that in Miriam Rooth "theatricality becomes virtually synonymous with prostitution" (Litvak 151).

[15] Nick later notices that "her tall upright black figure seemed in possession of the fair vastness like an exclamation point at the bottom of a blank page" (*TM* 187).

[16] For examples of this see *TM* pp. 105, 107, 109, 115, 473, 483, 545, 549.

[17] Sherringham also compares Miriam to Medusa:

> . . . "The Comic Muse? Never, never," Sherringham protested. "You're not to go smirking through the age and down to posterity—I'd rather see you as Medusa crowned with serpents. That's what you look like when you look your best." (*TM* 451-52)

Litvak, quoting a study by Neil Hertz, argues that the image of Medusa implies "snaky or phallic hair and the 'castration' of the female genitalia" (Litvak 159). But Litvak seems not to consider the fact that Medusa turned to stone all those who looked at her. Miriam, also, seems to have such an effect on her audience: Sherringham watches her with "an attentive but inexpressive silence" (*TM* 376). At another performance Nick is "struck by his dumbness" (*TM* 530): "He felt weak at the same time that he felt excited, and he felt excited at the same time that he knew or believed he knew that his face was a blank" (*TM* 534).

[18] A brief summary of the foundations of this idea will perhaps be useful here. A peculiarity of our understanding, Kant writes in the *Third Critique*, is that it "must proceed from the *analytically universal* to the particular" (Kant 291). This means that we only understand a universal by comparing it with something else on the basis of some common unit, the particular. The process of understanding Kant describes is one of apprehension and comprehension: we apprehend an object of nature by estimating its relative magnitude mathematically, and we comprehend it by estimating its magnitude aesthetically, i.e. my making a subjective determination of its magnitude. The sublime is a feeling of helplessness that arises when we cannot understand something: we apprehend it, but we cannot comprehend it because we cannot compare it with anything. Kant's mathematical sublime is sublime because it involves magnitudes that are too large to be measured: "We call *sublime* what is *absolutely large*" (Kant 103); "*That is sublime in comparison with which everything else is small*" (Kant 105). The sublime is thus the discomfort we feel when we apprehend something too big to comprehend, like a mountain or a storm, the implications of which are too immense for the mind to categorize. The sublime, as

an effect of the process of measuring, is peculiar because it is experienced over time. It is endless. Kant discusses this unpleasant feeling at length in §27:

> Measuring (as [a way of] apprehending) a space is at the same time describing it, and hence it is an objective movement in the imagination and a progression. On the other hand, comprehending a multiplicity in a unity (of intuition rather than thought), and hence comprehending in one instant what is apprehended successively, is a regression that in turn cancels the condition of time in the imagination's progression and makes *simultaneity* intuitable. Hence, (since temporal succession is a condition of the inner sense and of an intuition) it is a subjective movement of the imagination by which it does violence to the inner sense, and this violence must be the more significant the larger the quantum is that the imagination comprehends in one intuition. Hence the effort to take up into a single intuition a measure for magnitude requiring a significant time for apprehension is a way of presenting which subjectively considered is contrapurposive, but which objectively is needed to estimate magnitude and hence is purposive. And yet this same violence that the imagination inflicts on the subject is still judged purposive *for the whole vocation* of the mind. (Kant 116)

The mathematical sublime, then, is violence to the inner sense, and it is easy to see how well this applies to Miriam Rooth's effect on Peter Sherringham. Though Miriam Rooth is not large in stature she has a certain vastness of person much like that James was later to impute to Maud Lowder in *The Wings of the Dove*. This aesthetic largeness has much the same violent effect on Peter as the hugeness Kant has in mind in describing the mathematical sublime (see note 30 below). This violence, Kant writes, while subjectively contrapurposive, is objectively purposive because the process of trying to comprehend a multiplicity in a unity is the only way of approaching things that are too large to comprehend in a single act. The violence results from the demand upon the understanding to comprehend something that it can only apprehend, but since we want to comprehend these immense objects, the violence is both painful and exciting. Comprehension of great magnitudes is painful, and takes time, and the sublime is alluring because of this new dimension of time. It is a feeling of endlessness, of eternity, and of terror.

The sublime, unlike beauty, is a feeling, and is not an attribute that individual objects can possess inherently:

> true sublime must be sought only in the mind of the judging person, not in the natural object the judging of which prompts this mental attunement. (Kant 113)

Thus the only 'thing' that is itself sublime is reason itself, or God. But many things in nature seem sublime, i.e. they arouse the feeling of the sublime, and it is the nature of this seeming that I am concerned with here. In investigating objects of beauty we search for a standard against which beauty can be measured. But for the sublime we require "a basis merely within ourselves and in the way of thinking that introduces sublimity into our presentation of nature" (Kant 100).

[19] This is because of what Kant sees as the fundamental difference between nature and art:

> Art is distinguished from nature as doing (*facere*) is from acting or operating in general (*agere*); and the product or result of art is distinguished from that of nature, the first being a work (*opus*), the second an effect (*effectus*). (Kant 170)

Miriam is thus not a mere effect but a work, one whose purpose is to produce effects.

20 I take *The Tragic Muse* as proof that James became not only more tolerant of but fascinated by "brute sublimity" over time, just as he did to a lesser extent with Whitman himself.

21 Jean-François Lyotard has linked the sublime with modernism in his essay "What is Postmodernism?" He distinguishes two "modes" of aesthetic expression in modernity. The first, modernism, emphasizes either "the powerlessness of the faculty of presentation" or "the power of the faculty to conceive," the two moments of the sublime, and the second stresses "the increase of being and the jubilation which result from the invention of new rules" of postmodernism (Lyotard 79-80). The first, in other words, is sublime because it aspires to a presentation of the unpresentable:

> We have an Idea of the world (the totality of what is) but we do not have the capacity to show an example of it. We have the Idea of the simple (that which cannot be broken, decomposed) but we cannot illustrate it with a sensible object which would be a 'case' of it. (Lyotard 78)

22 James's heroine, in her sublimity, bears a great resemblance to William Russell's Tragic Muse. Russell's "The Tragic Muse: A Poem. Addressed to Mrs. Siddons" (1783) describes the actress as "Sublimely seated on the Tragic Throne" in its dedication. The poem attempts to show that Mrs. Siddons is to be exalted in spite of the baseness of her profession. Russell's Muse, like James's, is "born to give delight" (Russell l. 9; cf. *TM* 269), and like her Miriam is "drawn so true / that Beauty's self with terror strikes the view" (Russell ll. 47-48). In Miriam, too, "Pleasure rises from the shock of Pain" (Russell l. 75), and Peter Sherringham, like the poet in Russell's poem, seems to want to wail:

> —O Siddons, cease to strain
> The nerve on Pleasure on the rack of Pain:
> It thrills already in divine excess!
> Yet fondly we the fair Tormentor bless,
> And woo her to prolong our exquisite distress.
> (Russell, *The Tragic Muse*, ll. 167-71)

It seems unlikely that James would have known this poem directly, but the coincidences between the treatment of the actress in Russell's poem and James's novel indicate a long tradition of the connection between the theater and the sublime.

23 Note James's approval of this renunciation in the Preface: "There need never, at the worst, be any doubt about the things advantageously chuckable for art; the question is all but of choosing them in the heap" (*AN* 82).

24 I suggest that Nick's first painting of Miriam Rooth can be compared with Sir Joshua Reynolds' *Mrs. Siddons as The Tragic Muse*, the source of the title of James's novel. In this painting the famous actress sits on her throne gazing to her right and up into space. Though Reynolds' painting is realistic rather than impressionistic it is a poetic painting with a graceful arabesque that gives it the purity and serenity of a perfect tribute to the classical ideal. Like Gérôme's portrait of Rachel, which in James's novel portrays the great French actress "with the antique attributes of tragedy" (*TM* 281), Reynolds' Tragic Muse is flanked from behind by two murky

figures, bearing the emblematic cup and dagger of the muse of tragedy (Robert Falk has convincingly suggested that these two figures are represented in James's novel by Nick Dormer and Peter Sherringham). Reynolds' own reproduction of this painting is reproduced in Nicholas Penny's *Reynolds*; see also David Mannings' history of the work on pages 324-26 of the same volume. According to Mannings, Reynolds may have taken the idea of representing Mrs. Siddons as the Tragic Muse from a poem by William Russell entitled "The Tragic Muse: A Poem Addressed to Mrs Siddons"—see note 22 above.

[25] This tension between art and life is also similar to that between word and image in Michel Foucault's *This is Not a Pipe* (an analysis of Magritte's painting of the same name):

> By resemblance we demonstrate and speak across difference: The two systems can neither merge nor intersect. In one way or another, subordination is required. Either the text is ruled by the image (as in those paintings where a book, an inscription, a letter, or the name of a person are represented); or else the image is ruled by the text (as in books where a drawing completes, as if it were merely taking a short cut, the message that the words are charged to represent. (Foucault 32)

[26] For an illustration of art work acting as a frame and frames acting as the work, see the engraving reproduced on *TP* 72.

[27] *The Winter's Tale* V.iii.99.

[28] Note that dishonesty is the charge she brings against Peter: "You're dishonest, you're ungrateful, you're false!" (*TM* 546).

[29]
> Who would fardels bare,
> To grunt and sweat under a weary life,
> But that the dread of something after death,
> The undiscovered country, from whose bourn
> No traveller returns, puzzles the will,
> And makes us rather bear those ills we have
> Than fly to others that we know not of?
> *Hamlet* III.i.76-82

[30] One of the few examples of sublime art Kant gives is that of the pyramids of Egypt:

> one must neither get too close to them nor stay too far away. For if one stays too far away, then the apprehended parts (the stones on top of one another) are presented only obscurely, and hence their presentation has no effect on the subject's aesthetic judgment; and if one gets too close, then the eye needs some time to complete the apprehension from the base to the peak, but during that time some of the earlier parts are invariably extinguished in the imagination before it has apprehended the later ones, and hence the comprehension is never complete. (Kant 108)

[31] It is appropriate, of course, that Nick should attempt to create a sublime work in which two art forms are combined:

> He was conscious of a double nature; there were two men in him, quite separate, whose leading features had little in common and each of whom insisted on having an independent turn at life. (*TM* 204)

It is clear that his portrait of Julia, if he ever has the chance to paint it, will be even more sublime yet:

> [Biddy] didn't see his face in that movement, but an observer to whom it had been presented might have fancied that it denoted a foreboding that was not exactly a dread, yet was not exclusively a joy. (*TM* 604)

NOTES TO CHAPTER II

1 *TP* 63.

2 Jones, 112.

3 Cf. Felman, 120.

4 Derrida goes on to explain this formulation, which in the French reads "*Il est d'abord l'à-bord*":

> If we wanted to play a little—for the sake of poetics—at etymology, the *à-bord* would refer us to the Middle High German bort (table, plank, deck of a vessel). "The *bord* is thus properly speaking a plank; and etymology allows us to grasp the ways its meanings link together. The primary meaning is the deck of a vessel, i.e. a construction of planks; then, by metonymy, that which borders, that which encloses, hat which limits, that which is at the extremity." Says Littré. (*TP* 54)

5 James clearly felt that it was important that both these effects of the frame happen together and that they did not happen together for Nathaniel Hawthorne. In an 1872 review of an edition of Hawthorne's journals from his travels to France and Italy, James discusses the "admirably honest" (*LC* 310) and "natural" (*LC* 309) genius, whose response to the European paintings he finds charmingly naive:

> The "most delicate charm" to Mr. Hawthorne was apparently simply the primal freshness and brightness of paint and varnish, and—not to put too fine a point on it—the new gilding of the frame. (*LC* 311)

In another essay on Hawthorne (1879), James writes:

> Whenever he talks of statues he makes a great point of the smoothness and whiteness of the marble—speaks of the surface of the marble as if it were half the beauty of the image; and when he discourses of pictures, one feels that the brightness and dinginess of the frame is an essential part of his impression of the work. (*LC* 441)

James found Hawthorne's uneducated American naivete amusing because of its attention to surface detail, particularly that of the frame, to the exclusion of the work itself. His patient chiding shows how important it was for him, that the frame be a part of the whole painting, a part that works with the work instead of distracting attention from it. The frame must accentuate the work by eliminating itself, by disappearing from the viewer's field of vision.

6 See Peter G. Beidler, Chapter 2, for some of the ones that James might have been familiar with.

7 "The Way it Came," later renamed "The Friends of the Friends," is another ghost story written just before *The Turn of the Screw*, and it is framed in much the same way as the latter. The tale's prologue (*CT*, v. IX, p. 371) takes the form of a letter from

an editor to a possible publisher addressing the question of "the possibility of publication" of a manuscript, a copy of which follows. The story, divided by the narrator "for your convenience into several short chapters" but otherwise unaltered, is judged to be flawed. Rather than repairing it, however, the narrator prefaces the story with a cover letter of explanation, which acts as a wheelchair or frame. This principle of adding rather than altering is the same one at work in *The Turn of the Screw.*

[8] Peter G. Beidler, in *Ghosts, Demons and Henry James,* has suggested that Douglas, in his college days, was a member of the Cambridge Ghost Club, and that "it may have been at Douglas's urging that the governess made a written statement of her experiences" (Beidler 40). This suggestion, as Beidler notes, would account for a number of inconsistencies in the novel, the confessional tone of the narrative among them.

[9] It is necessary to point out that the propaedeutic pre-chapter to *What Maisie Knew,* James's "ugly little comedy" (*NB* 167), is not a parergonal frame like the Prologue to *The Turn of the Screw.* The Prologue to *What Maisie Knew,* it is true, differs in tone and style from the narrative that follows it. Mary Galbraith, furthermore, has analyzed the transition from the Prologue to Chapter 1 of the novel and shown that the Prologue differs epistemologically as well. In the Prologue, Maisie does not yet exist as a character but only as a "marker" in the adults' game:

> The last paragraph of the prologue is almost entirely devoted to the perspective of [Beale and Ida's] social circle, for whom the Faranges's divorce is a wonderful distraction. The topics of paragraph 7 [of the Prologue] enact the topics of importance to this circle: physical appearance and money. Within this universe, the child Maisie is virtually nonexistent as is evidenced by the lack of mention of her within this paragraph. She exists only as a marker in the game of wealth, beauty, and power. (Galbraith 199)

Maisie, as Galbraith illustrates, is brought to life only by the first sentence of Chapter 1. Even this difference between Prologue and tale, however, does not make the Prologue a frame. The Prologue is simply a part of the novel that comes before the first chapter. It is an introduction, an informative beginning, exactly the likes of which *The Turn of the Screw* is lacking. The fact that the Prologue to *What Maisie Knew* precedes the first chapter of the novel emphasizes the beginning of the novel rather than obfuscating it as is the case in *The Turn of the Screw.*

[10] See the Notebook entry for Saturday, January 12, 1895.

[11] Cf. Shoshana Felman's account of the mechanics of letter-writing in *The Turn of the Screw* in ch. 5 of her "Turning the Screw of Interpretation."

[12] Michael Taylor has interestingly suggested that the reason for this respect is that the narrator is female, but in any case the mysterious relation emphasizes the dramatic element of the Prologue and heightens the contrast with the governess's narrative.

[13] This should not be surprising from a writer who attempted to fuse speech and writing together with dictation. In a letter to his friend Mary Cadwalader Jones (Oct. 23, 1902), James defended his practice of writing through an amanuensis:

> It soon enough, accordingly, becomes, *intellectually,* absolutely identical with the act of writing. . . . (*WD* 454)

[1] *TP* 54.

[2] James heard the story that became *The Turn of the Screw* on Thursday, January 10, 1895, according to the notebook entry of the following Saturday, but he did not publish the story until January of 1898 (*NB* 109). James got the idea for *What Maisie Knew* on November 12, 1892, according to his note dated two days later, and it was published in 1897.

[3] Sir Claude, originally "the Captain," is described as "a simple, good, mild chap" in the *Notebooks.* See the entry for December 22, 1895 (*NB* 150).

[4] "'Poor little monkey!' [the good lady] at last exclaimed; and the words were an epitaph for the tomb of Maisie's childhood." (*What Maisie Knew* 36)

[5] See, for example, this famous description:

> [Maisie's] features had somehow become prominent; they were so perpetually nipped by the gentlemen who came to see her father and the smoke of whose cigarettes went into her face. Some of these men made her strike matches and light their cigarettes; others, holding her on knees violently jolted, pinched the calves of her legs till she shrieked—her shriek was much admired—and reproached them with being toothpicks. The word stuck in her mind and contributed to her feeling from this time that she was deficient in something that would meet the general desire. She found out what it was; it was a congenital tendency to the production of a substance to which Moddle, her nurse, gave a short ugly name, a name painfully associated at dinner with the part of the joint that she didn't like. (*WMK* 39-40)

[6] Ida Farange's interest in her daughter is reduced to "the mere maternal pull" (*WMK*).

[7] Though the Penguin edition of *What Maisie Knew* uses a free-standing hyphen to separate these phrases, I will use in my transcriptions the double dash employed by the editors of the Norton Critical editions of James's novels. Evidence that the double dash is more in line with James's own intentions is to be found in Book Five of *The Ambassadors,* just after Strether's famous "Live all you can" speech:

> Slowly and sociably, with full pauses and straight dashes, Strether had so delivered himself. (*TA* 132)

[8] Foster notes that "her analysis of the lovers goes beyond understanding them, beyond knowing about love, to a participation in love's stratagems" (Foster 209).

[9] James repeatedly calls Mrs Wix an "honest frump" in the Notebooks—see the entry for December 22, 1895 (*NB* 149). Mrs Wix follows Maisie wherever she goes, appearing later, to Maisie, on the cliffs of Dover the night before Maisie and Sir Claude break for France:

> Maisie stared at them as if she might really make out after a little a queer dear figure perched on them—a figure as to which she had already the subtle sense that, wherever perched, it would be the very oddest yet seen in France. But it was at least as exciting to feel where Mrs Wix wasn't as it would have been to know where she was. (*WMK* 165-66)

[10] Marriage in *What Maisie Knew* is simply "the unbroken opportunity to quarrel" (*WMK* 37).

[11] James writes in the Preface that "the child becoming a centre and pretext for a fresh system of misbehaviour, a system moreover of a nature to spread and ramify: *there* would be the 'full' irony, there the promising theme into which the hint I had originally picked up would logically flower" (*WMK* 25).

[12] James writes in the Preface to *What Maisie Knew* that "the thing has but to become a part of the child's bewilderment for these small sterilities to drop from it and for the *scene* to emerge and prevail—vivid, special, wrought hard, to the hardness of the unforgettable; the scene that is exactly what Beale and Ida and Mrs Cuddon, and even Sir Claude and Mrs Beale, would never for a moment have succeeded in making their scant unredeemed importances—namely *appreciable*" (*WMK* 29-30). Maisie's role as a frame, then, is not only to make her parents' and stepparents' adultery appear decent to their peers in society, but also to validate their presentation to the reader by making them "*appreciable.*" It is Maisie's unifying presence that makes her upbringing what Lambert Strether calls a "situation" (*TA* 168) or "case" (*TA* 234); it is she alone that makes her milieu interesting. Being "appreciable" is the aesthetic ideal that I will focus on in the next chapter.

[13] Armstrong observes that "the excess of seeing over understanding which imprisons Maisie in a world of ambiguity is the surplus of her unreflective experience over what she can appropriate in reflection" (Armstrong 519). Thomas Jeffers, in a similar vein, has described Maisie's childhood as a tomb: "If the denouement signals 'the death of her childhood, properly speaking' (*WMK* 28), it is the death of something deathly. Denied all salutary light and air, Maisie's childhood has been buried in 'the tomb' (*WMK* 36)" (Jeffers 161). [I have adjusted Jeffers's pagination to correspond to that of the Penguin edition.]

[14] This is perhaps the place to mention that a whole chapter could be probably written on the relevance to *What Maisie Knew* of Derrida's "Cartouches," the third essay in *The Truth in Painting*. "Cartouches" deals with a series of 127 drawings by Gérard Titus-Carmel. The drawings all portray a tiny coffin built by the artist, and Derrida's work explores the relationship of this paradigm to the series it engendered. This little coffin, which Derrida here describes as a male entity, is both necessary to the set of drawings (they are drawings of it) and

> fallen, destitute, neglected debris, *banished*, excluded from a family (tribe, people, *genos*) with which he no longer has any relationship. (*TP* 188)

Like Maisie, the paradigmatic coffin is

> an out-of-series (or outlaw) among others, in the law of the series, neither bigger nor smaller than each and every one, subtracted from all hierarchies, an effect of a series without family. (*TP* 221)

"Restitutions," which follows, a "'polylogue' (for n + 1—female—voices)" that deconstructs a dialogue between Martin Heidegger and Meyer Shapiro about Van Gogh's shoes, is also relevant (though the parallel here is less accurate):

> Do [the shoes in the painting] not have as their "principal" subject this time *the parergon*, all by itself, with all the consequences that follow from that? A *parergon* without *ergon*? A "pure" supplement? An article of clothing as a "naked" supplement to the "naked"? A supplement with nothing to supplement, calling, on the contrary, for what it supplements, to be its own supplement? (*TP* 302)

[15] Paul Theroux has noted the change in tone in Chapter 17 and postulated that it is here that James surrendered to his writer's cramp and began dictating to an amanuensis. See page 11 of Theroux's introduction to the Penguin edition.

[16] See the notebook entry for August 26, 1893 (*NB* 77).

[17] There is no extended dialogue until Chapter 6 and little of much importance until before Chapter 13.

[18] His stick, of course, is in Mrs Beale's bedroom (*WMK* 239).

[19] Foster writes: "Nothing in Maisie's experience makes it self-evident that taking a wealthy lover is evil. For Mrs. Wix, the leap from paying lovers to immorality is automatic, having been schooled for so long in a convention linking the two that she has come to assume it is a fact of nature. So long as Maisie has not learned this convention, her failure to follow Mrs. Wix's leap emphasizes the weakness of the logic of morality" (Foster 210).

NOTES TO CHAPTER IV

[1] *TP* 54.

[2] Strether also paints a "picture" (*TA* 50) of Mrs. Newsome for Maria Gostrey at every opportunity in the dawn of their acquaintance, and through his descriptions Miss Gostrey "sees" the subject of the painting: "how intensely you make me see her!" she exclaims to Strether (*TA* 50). Strether, as a frame connected to but on a different plane of existence than the work he is employed to serve, cannot see completely either his subject or the nature of his relationship to her, but Maria Gostrey is a seer, an observer and interpreter in the system of ill-detachable detachment that is Strether's situation:

> "You see more in it," he presently returned, "than I."
> "Of course I see *you* in it."
> "Well then you see more in 'me'!"
> "Than you see in yourself? Very likely. That's always one's right." (*TA* 53)

[3] Note Strether's similarity to Maisie in the following description:

> "he was being, as he constantly put it though mutely expressed it, used. He was as far as ever from making out exactly to what end; but he was none the less constantly accompanied by a sense of the service he rendered. He conceived only that this service was highly agreeable to those who profited by it; and he was indeed still waiting for the moment at which he should catch it in the act of proving disagreeable, proving in some degree intolerable, to himself. He failed to see how his situation could clear up at all logically except by some turn of events that would give him the pretext of disgust." (*TA* 152)

[4] See chapter three, note 12 above.

[5] R. W. Short has written that the theatrical images in *The Ambassadors* generally "stand for the unnatural, the meretricious, the over-ingenious, the glittering front, the false ritual, the social perversion" (Short 951) while Lodge has pointed out that "the legitimate theater is in fact one of the novel's touchstones for indicating fineness of crudity of sensibility, the acceptance or rejection of European culture and the idea of social beauty" (Lodge 210).

[6] Rivkin also seductively suggests that "her name falls one consonant short of 'go straight' and leaves us with the open-ended sound and open path of 'go stray'" (824).

[7] See also Holder-Barell 117-24.

[8] Garis has written that "there has in fact been no education at all" and that the novel's conclusion illustrates "Strether's incapacity for either education or life" (307). Goetz writes, similarly, that

> Maria's praise for [Strether's] imagination [at the end of chapter 29] comes at an ironic moment, just preceding Strether's retreat into the Lambinet-like French countryside where his imagination sets him up for his greatest fall in the novel, a fall which will almost wreck him. (Goetz 190).

I argue, however, that Strether's imaginative adventure almost saves him. To save him any further would violate the realism of the novel.

[9] William R. Goetz argues that in *The Ambassadors* a tension builds up between Strether and the narrator as a result of James's fear that Strether would too much resemble himself, making the book appear to be an autobiography. Goetz's thesis is based on James's famous renunciation of the first-person address in the Preface to *The Ambassadors*:

> Strether, . . . encaged and provided for as "The Ambassadors" encages and provides, has to keep in view proprieties much stiffer and more salutary than any our stiff and credulous gape are likely to bring home to him, has exhibitional conditions to meet, in a word, that forbid the terrible *fluidity* of self-revelation. (*TA* 11)

Goetz writes that the purpose of the Preface is to "make the avoidance of autobiography seem a purely technical decision" (Goetz 185) but that this avoidance is really an act of defense, and that Strether is guilty of the crime of impersonating his own creator. Strether's encagement within the text, Goetz writes, functions as punishment for this crime:

> The familiar tightness versus fluidity operates here in a way uncomfortable to Strether. He is encaged and subject to the "stiffer proprieties" of James's focalized narrative so that he cannot escape the fictional bounds of the text and be confused with his author. (Goetz 187)

Goetz perceives the obvious resemblance between James and Strether as one that made the former uneasy and writes that "this obvious threat of the author's identification with his hero calls forth a countermovement, an act that will protect James by keeping Strether distinct from him, a prisoner, as it were, of the fictional text" (Goetz 187). Goetz sees Strether's imprisonment, in other words, as an act of defense on the part of tyrannical author who refuses him "the double privilege of subject and object" (*TA* 11) to protect himself from the indignity of autobiography. I think that it is precisely this tyranny that Strether escapes from in the Lambinet chapters.

[10] The Preface to *The Ambassadors* shows James more confident than at any other point in *The Art of the Novel*, and the metaphor he chooses to convey his "excitement," that of the pursuit of a run-away slave, shows the extent of his confidence in his achievement:

> No privilege of the teller of tales and the handler of puppets is more delightful, or has more of the suspense and the thrill of a game of difficulty breathlessly

> played, than just this business of looking for the unseen and the occult, in a scheme half-grasped, by the light or, so to speak, by the clinging scent, of the gage already in hand. No dreadful old pursuit of the hidden slave with bloodhounds and the rag of association can ever, for "excitement," I judge, have bettered it at its best. (*TA* 4)

One wonders, then, what Derrida has in mind when he asks us to "Witness the boredom experienced by Henry James while writing the prefaces to his complete works at the end of his life" (*D* 27, note 27).

[11] Viola Hopkins has suggested that Strether, by this point, has drifted out of Lambinet's "French ruralism" into something more impressionistic, a Manet perhaps. See Hopkins 565.

[12] Preface to *The American* (*AN* 24).

WORKS CITED

WORKS BY HENRY JAMES

Henry James. *Henry James: Literary Criticism*, ed. L. Edel (New York: Literary Classics of the United States, 1984).

———. "John Singer Sargent." *Harper's New Monthly Magazine* 75 (1887): 683-91.

———. *The Awkward Age*, ed. R. Blythe and P. Crick (Harmondsworth: Penguin, 1987).

———. *The Art of the Novel*, ed. R. P. Blackmur (New York: Charles Scribner's Sons, 1934).

———. "The Altar of the Dead," in L. Edel, ed., *The Complete Tales of Henry James*, v. IX: 1892-1898 (New York: J. B. Lippincott, 1964) 231-71.

———. *The Ambassadors*, ed. S. P. Rosembaum (New York: Norton, 1964).

———. *The Complete Notebooks of Henry James*, ed. L. Edel and L. Powers (New York: Oxford UP, 1987).

———. *The Tragic Muse*, ed. L. Edel (New York: Harper & Brothers, 1960).

———. *The Turn of the Screw*, ed. Robert Kimbrough (New York: Norton, 1966).

———. "The Way it Came," in L. Edel, ed., *The Complete Tales of Henry James*, v. IX: 1892-1898 (New York: J. B. Lippincott, 1964) 371-401.

———. *The Wings of the Dove*, ed. J. D. Crowley and R. A. Hocks (New York: Norton, 1978).

———. *What Maisie Knew*, ed. P. Theroux and P. Crick (London: Penguin Books, 1985).

OTHER WORKS CITED

Abbott, Reginald. "The Incredible Floating Man: Henry James's Lambert Strether." *Henry James Review* 11 (1990): 176-88.

Armstrong, Paul B. "How Maisie Knows: The Phenomenology of James's Moral Vision." *Texas Studies in Literature and Language* 20 (1978): 517-37.

Beidler, Peter G. *Ghosts, Demons and Henry James:* The Turn of the Screw *at the Turn of the Century*. U of Missouri P, 1989.

Bellringer, Alan W. "*The Tragic Muse*: 'The Objective Centre.'" *Journal of American Studies* 4 (1970): 73-89.

Blackall, Jean Frantz. "Moral Geography in *What Maisie Knew*." *University of Toronto Quarterly* 48 (1978-79): 130-48.

Caws, Mary Ann. *Reading Frames in Modern Fiction.* Princeton UP, 1985.

Crowl, Susan. "Aesthetic Allegory in *The Turn of the Screw.*" *Novel* 4 (1971): 107-22.

Derrida, Jacques. *Dissemination.* Trans. and Ed. Barbara Johnson. U of Chicago P, 1981.

———. "Economimesis." *Diacritics* 11 (1981): 3-25.

———. *Of Grammatology.* Trans. G. C. Spivak. Johns Hopkins UP, 1974.

———. *Spurs: Nietzsche's Styles.* Trans. B. Harlow. U of Chicago P, 1979.

———. "The Other Heading: Memories, Responses, and Responsibilities." *PMLA* 108 (1993): 89-93.

———. *The Truth in Painting.* Trans. G. Bennington and I. McLeod. U of Chicago P, 1987.

Edel, Leon. "The Point of View." *The Turn of the Screw,* ed. R. Kimbrough. New York: Norton, 1966. 228-34.

Falk, Robert. "*The Tragic Muse*: Henry James's Loosest, Baggiest Novel?" *Themes and Directions in American Literature, Essays in Honor of Leon Howard.* R. Browne and D. Pizer, eds. Lafayette, Indiana: Purdue U Studies (1969): 148-62.

Felman, Shoshana. "Turning the Screw of Interpretation." *Yale French Studies* 55/56 (1978): 94-207.

Foster, Dennis. "Maisie Supposed to Know: Amo(u)ral Analysis." *Henry James Review* 5 (1984): 207-16

Foucault, Michel. *This is Not a Pipe.* Trans. J. Harkness. Berkeley: Quantum, 1982.

Fried, Michael. "Art and Objecthood," in *Minimal Art: A Critical Anthology,* ed. G. Battcock (New York: Dutton, 1968) 116-47.

Frye, Northrop. *Anatomy of Criticism.* Princeton UP, 1957.

Galbraith, Mary. "What Everybody Knew Versus What Maisie Knew: The Change in Epistemological Perspective from the Prologue to the Opening of Chapter 1 in *What Maisie Knew.*" *Style* 23 (1989): 197-212.

Garis, Robert E. "The Two Lambert Strethers: A New Reading of *The Ambassadors.*" *Modern Fiction Studies* 7 (1961-62): 305-16.

Goetz, William R. "The Allegory of Representation in *The Tragic Muse.*" *Journal of Narrative Technique* 8 (1978): 151-64.

———. *Henry James and the Darkest Abyss of Romance.* Baton Rouge: Louisiana State UP, 1986.

———. "The '*Frame*' of *The Turn of the Screw*: Framing the Reader In." *Studies in Short Fiction* 18 (1988): 71-74.

Heidegger, Martin. *Poetry, Language, Thought.* New York: Harper and Row, 1975.

Holder-Barrell, Alexander. *The Developement of Imagery and its Functional Significance in Henry James's Novels.* Basel, 1959.

Hopkins, Viola. "Visual Art Devices and Parallels in the Fiction of Henry James." *PMLA* 76 (1961): 561-74.

Jeffers, Thomas L. "Maisie's Moral Sense: Finding Out for Herself." *Nineteenth-Century Fiction* 34 (1979): 154-72.

Jones, Alexander E. "Point of View in *The Turn of the Screw.*" *PMLA* 74 (1959): 112-22.

Kant, Immanuel. *Critique of Judgment.* Trans. Werner S. Pluhar. Indianapolis: Hackett Publishing Company, 1987.

Litvak, Joseph. "Actress, Monster, Novelist: *The Tragic Muse* as a Novel of Theatricality." *Texas Studies in Language and Literature* 29 (1987): 141-68.

Lodge, David. *Language of Fiction: Essays in Criticism and Verbal Analysis of the English Novel.* New York: Columbia UP, 1966.

Lyotard, Jean-François. *The Postmodern Condition: A Report on Knowledge.* Minneapolis: University of Minnesota Press, 1979.

McMaster, Graham. "Henry James and India: A Historical Reading of *The Turn of the Screw.*" *CLIO* 18 (1988): 23-40.

Nietzsche, Friedrich. *The Will to Power.* Trans. W. Kaufman and R. J. Hollingdale. New York: Vintage, 1968.

Paglia, Camille. *Sexual Personae.* New York: Vintage, 1991.

Penny, Nicholas, et al. *Reynolds.* New York: Harry N. Abrams, 1986.

Rivkin, Julie. "The Logic of Delegation in *The Ambassadors.*" *PMLA* 101 (1986): 819-31.

Rowe, John Carlos. *The Theoretical Dimensions of Henry James.* Madison: The University of Wisconsin Press, 1984, ch. 4.

Russell, William. "The Tragic Muse: A Poem. Addressed to Mrs. Siddons." London: printed for G. Kearsley, 1783.

Rust, Richard Dilworth. "Liminality in *The Turn of the Screw.*" *Studies in Short Fiction* 25 (1988): 441-46.

Short, R. W. "Henry James's World of Images." *PMLA* 68 (1953): 943-60.

Spilka, Mark. "'The Art of Fiction' Controversy." *Towards a Poetics of Fiction.* Ed. Mark Spilka. Bloomington and London: Indiana UP, 1977.

Sternberg, Meir. "Spatiotemporal Art and the Other Henry James: The Case of *The Tragic Muse.*" *Poetics Today* 5 (1984): 755-830.

Taylor, Michael J. H. "A Note on the First Narrator of 'The Turn of the Screw.'" *American Literature* 53 (1982): 717-22.

Ward, J. A. "The Portraits of Henry James." *Henry James Review* 10 (1989): 1-14.

Wegelin, Christof. "The Lesson of Social Beauty." *The Turn of the Screw.* Ed. R. Kimbrough. New York: Norton, 1966: 442-58.

Wise, James N. "The Floating World of Lambert Strether." *Arlington Quarterly* 2 (1969): 80-110.